PROPERTY OF
CHURCH OF
LIBRARY

D0466729

ACRES OF HOPE

*The Miraculous Story
of One Family's Gift of Love
to Children without Hope*

Patty Anglin
with Joe Musser

PROMISE
PRESS
An Imprint of Barbour Publishing

©1999 by Patty Anglin

ISBN 1-57748-625-0

All rights reserved. No part of this publication may be reproduced or transmitted in any form or by any means without written permission of the publisher.

Published by Promise Press, an imprint of Barbour Publishing, Inc., P.O. Box 719, Uhrichsville, Ohio 44683
http://www.barbourbooks.com

 Member of the
Evangelical Christian
Publishers Association

Printed in the United States of America.

DEDICATION

This book is fondly dedicated to my mother, Jennie Lucille, who taught me compassion by her example. This book is also dedicated to all adoptive parents who have shown me compassion through their love for babies and children who need love and a "forever family." Furthermore, this book is dedicated to all the little children who are still very much in need of compassion.

CONTENTS

I've gotten used to being on display. Whether it's the child studying my wheelchair, the senior citizen across the way smiling sympathetically, or the waiter eyeing me carefully as I use my bent spoon to eat pieces of hamburger, I'm aware that people are watching. Some might watch out of pity, some out of admiration. All watch, I sense, with unspoken questions.

It's part of the territory that comes with a disability.

It's what the Anglin family faces everyday. But like the wonderful Anglin clan, a marvelously motley crew of kids, different heights and sizes, colors, abilities and disabilities, I choose to think that people's unspoken questions are, for the most part, good-natured. That's because Patty Anglin and I, as followers of Jesus Christ, are constrained to think the best of others. We are called to be on display (as any Christian is). We are encouraged by God's Word to smile from the inside out as the strength of God shows up bountifully through our physical limitations—even the severe limitations of a child like Zachary, born missing his lower arms and legs. When people eye us, I believe they are thinking, "How great the God of these people must be to inspire such faith and confidence."

Somehow, when the Anglin family all go out to Burger

King, I don't think they mind being on display. Their story inspires faith and confidence in people who observe them. Families are strengthened when they see the unity which binds the Anglins together. I feel the same.

I remember the first time I saw little Zachary. I hardly noticed what he lacked because of that smile which stretched from ear to ear. His happy-hearted disposition was no doubt borrowed from his mother, father, and his brothers and sisters.

The Anglin's story showcases 1 Corinthians 12:24–26 where we learn that, "God has combined the members of the body and has given greater honor to the parts that lacked it, so that there should be no division in the body, but that its parts should have equal concern for each other. If one part suffers, every part suffers with it; if one part is honored, every part rejoices with it."

The family whose biography you hold in your hands may have members who are lacking literal "parts," but the body is whole and complete. God has blessed them with the great honor of encouraging and strengthening the rest of the body of Christ.

This is what will strike you about *Acres of Hope*. From the first chapter to the last, your heart will be warmed as you read how the entire Anglin family has dealt with discouragement, impossible situations, discrimination, and physical limitations.

You will learn of a family whose soul is settled and whose peace is profound.

You will discover a mother and a father who lead, not with a heavy hand, but with a compassionate heart.

And like me, you will think "If this family can, by the grace of God, overcome its limitations, I can, too."

JONI EARECKSON TADA

President, Joni and Friends

Fall 1999

The opportunity for us to tell our story in a book happened in such an unusual way. We believe that God arranged the events and schedules of our lives and the lives of several other people to intersect at the exact time and place.

First, I took our baby Zachary to Florida for a brief visit with my mother while awaiting permission to bring Zack into Wisconsin where we live. It was there that I met and shared our experiences with Bill Barbour, a gracious man and neighbor of my mother. He told me that he had contacts with a Christian publishing company and wanted us to tell our story to a much wider audience.

However, I had no experience in writing a book but was told that someone could work with me to put the project together. In the same providence of God, a veteran author had contacted the publisher when another writing project had been delayed and he was looking for an assignment to fill his schedule. That author, Joe Musser, has written over thirty-five books, including the famous best-seller *Joni,* which sold over 3.5 million copies and was made into a major motion picture.

There are simply too many "coincidental" things about this book project that make me believe that it has a supernatural life of its own in the planning, writing, and production. I have come to believe that it's a story worth telling. So with the support and encouragement of the publishers, we have begun to write about what has turned out to be a most miraculous and exciting adventure.

We've tried to capture the significant events and remarkable experiences in this book.

Along the way you'll meet our seven biological children as well as our eight adopted kids. The story of our biological children is just as interesting and inspiring, but that's another book. This book is about the eight "special-needs" children that we have taken into our home and through adoption have made a permanent part of our family.

It is certainly not our wish in any way to compromise the privacy of our children or the privacy of their biological parents or families. Nor is it our intention to point accusing fingers at any faults or implied failings of any social services agencies. For that reason we have, in some instances, changed the names of some people and places. When that occurs we have footnoted the occurrence for the reader.

Because my husband Harold and I are the parents of fifteen children, we have experienced nearly every emotion of human experience and have run into all kinds of problems and suffering. Yet those troubles all pale in comparison to the myriad kinds of miracles and answers to prayer that we've also experienced.

It is our prayer that what has happened to us will challenge, inspire, and provoke you in some wonderful ways.

Patty Anglin

Ashland, Wisconsin

July 1999

CHAPTER ONE

African Roots

I thought I'd misunderstood the voice on the other end of the telephone. "What did you say?" I asked.

"It's true! The hospital nurse overheard them talking. She heard the father say that he was actually planning to *kill their newborn baby!*"

The hair on the back of my neck stood up as my mind tried to grasp the horror of such an act of violence.

The telephone call was from my friend, Margaret Fleming. Margaret is the director of Adopt Link, an adoption agency in Chicago that specializes in adoptions of African-American and biracial babies and children.

"Oh, Patty," Margaret continued, "this is a travesty!" Then as she explained I began to understand the story more clearly. A baby boy was born without lower arms and legs. The baby had a few other medical concerns as well, but otherwise appeared to be a strong and healthy little guy.

The baby's parents were Nigerian and had won the Nigerian national lottery, so that's why they were in the United States. While in America the mother learned that she was pregnant and so the baby was born in a Chicago hospital.

However, after the baby was born and the parents learned about his severe limb impairments, they became overwhelmed with grief. They knew that they would be expected to follow their cultural practices, and if they did, it would require a most difficult decision on their part.

That's when the nurse overheard the father order his wife to get dressed so that they could leave the hospital.

"But she can't leave now," the nurse explained. "Your wife has had a very difficult breech birth—she must stay until we make sure that her bleeding has stopped, at least overnight."

"No," the man said bluntly, "we must leave at once. It is the custom."

"Custom?" the nurse asked.

"When a baby is born like this, with deformities, it is an evil omen. The child must not be allowed to live."

"Uh—what exactly do you mean?" the nurse asked him. Astonished, she could hardly believe such a thing could happen in this day in America. "When you say that your baby must not be allowed to live, do you mean you are going to *kill him?*"

"Yes, it is a part of our culture," the man replied in a matter-of-fact way.

"But you can't do that in our country! That's murder! It's against the laws of our land," the nurse told him excitedly.

The couple seemed confused by the information, but the husband was quite firm in the decision to take his wife and the baby and leave the hospital. The baby's father left the room and left the ordeal of decision up to the mother (whose Nigerian name I later learned was Iyapo[1]). Iyapo was crying, almost as if it was clear that she did not want to be a part of the cultural decision to end the baby's life but must have felt that she had no choice.

When the nurse told her supervisor, a quick call was made to the Social Services agency and they quickly intervened. A welfare worker met with the Nigerian couple and explained U.S. laws and told the parents that they could not harm the baby in any way. After some dialogue, a compromise was worked out—the couple could leave, but *without* the baby. They surrendered the child to the adoption agency and gave up all their parental rights to their newborn son.

Those were the bizarre events that had preceded my urgent telephone call from Margaret. As she was telling

---

[1]The name means "many trials, many difficult situations."

me the story, my thoughts flashed back many years to my own time in Africa. I had gone as a girl with my parents who were medical missionaries to (what is now) the Republic of Congo. I knew it was the custom of many African tribes to sacrifice a baby born with severe birth defects. It is considered an evil omen—and it's always said to be the fault of the mother. Sometimes it is even thought that an evil spirit impregnated the mother in the first place. In any event, the baby is killed and the mother mutilates herself as part of the grieving process. It seemed strange to hear of such a thing happening in a modern city like Chicago, though.

"Patty, do you have any families on your list that might be willing to consider adopting this special-needs baby?" Margaret was asking as my mind came back from its mental detour to Africa.

I was surprised at the first words out of my mouth. "Margaret," I said, "of course I know of someone who will take this baby. You're talking about *my* son! *We'll* take him."

My husband Harold walked into the room just then and I put my hand over the phone and said to him, "Honey, our baby boy has just been born in Chicago."

Harold looked at me with a slightly odd expression, then smiled. "Really?" he said with a bemused expression that seemed to say, "Here we go again!"

He wouldn't be surprised. After all, this was certainly not the first child we'd be taking into our home. Harold and I are the parents of *fifteen children*—seven biological children and eight adopted kids.[1] So there's always room for one more.

Our family is sort of a mini-United Nations—with youngsters who are American, Hispanic, Indian, African, and African-American. In between having our own children and adopting, we were also foster parents to more children than I can remember—at least several dozen— including a number of medically challenged, drug-exposed, fragile babies, and special-needs children.

My own preparation for caring for children began as a young girl. I was the second oldest daughter born to missionary parents. My dad, Dr. Richard Pelham, was the pastor of several churches in the East while he put himself through medical school. During that time my father was pastor for churches in New Jersey, Pennsylvania, and Flint, Michigan, which I remember as our first "real" home. Then Daddy took our family to Africa as medical missionaries in the 1960s.

Dad was a hardworking, goal-driven man who felt he was making a real difference in Africa. As a surgeon for the American Baptist mission hospital, he always had a full schedule of work in his operating room. And in the rare times he wasn't operating, he was likely to be

---

[1]Harold had four children and I had two in our previous marriages. We are the parents of T. J. who was born before we adopted our eight special-needs children.

preaching in an African village church. As a result, he wasn't always available when I wanted or needed him.

Mother was absolutely devoted to God, as well as to her husband and family, almost to the point that she had no identity of her own. She was a missionary, wife of Dr. Pelham, and mother to Amy, Patty, Becca, and Stephen. Mother was the most unselfish person I have ever known and she greatly influenced my own values and beliefs.

I was nine years old when I understood the gospel message and asked Jesus Christ to come into my heart. I was fortified with the reality of this new birth as our family arrived in Africa, and I prayed that God would show me how even a nine-year-old could serve Him.

However, this vast country and its strange, often mysterious culture overwhelmed me. My sister, Amy, was two years older and adapted more quickly than I did. When we were sent off to the boarding school for missionary kids, Amy made friends quickly and easily. By then I was about ten years old and not used to being away from home. I grew homesick right away.

To make matters worse, those were years of puberty for me and no one was there to explain what was happening to me when I had my first menstrual period. The transition from our small close-knit family in America to a far-flung household spread between hospital, home, and boarding school (with so many other people) was difficult.

The Tasok Boarding School began as a missionary educational institution and later became an international school, yet it still mostly served children of career missionaries. We lived in the Baptist hostel with forty-five other Baptist missionary kids. There were also quite a few other denominations—Methodists, Presbyterians, and Christian and Missionary Alliance. Each denomination had its own hostel, with up to about fifty kids from each of these denominations enrolled in the Tasok school.

In our hostel there was a girls' hall and a boys' hall. An unmarried woman supervised the girls and a married couple supervised the boys, as well as managed the Baptist hostel. I remember being afraid and lonely those first weeks. It was good having Amy at the school for reassurance, but I rarely saw her. She had volunteered to be "big sister" to the really young children of seven and eight years old. They, like me, were having a tough time being away from their parents. With Amy away in the "little kids' hall" I was always homesick and lonely.

Fortunately, there were a lot of fun activities to help take my mind off my loneliness. Every Tuesday we were taken to the statue overlooking the Congo River—depicting the journalist Henry Stanley (whose search found the famous missionary David Livingston). The children would climb on the statue and after running, games, and other fun we'd have a picnic.

On Saturdays our group was taken to the river to swim. It was always a lot of fun and even today I miss those experiences.

Despite the fun, however, the school itself was hard for me. In addition to my loneliness and homesickness, I had great difficulty learning. School was a struggle. While the other kids seemed to be able to read with ease, I stumbled over what seemed to me an incomprehensible puzzle—seeing words on the page that were out of place. I had trouble distinguishing "bad" from "dab," or similar pairings of words. My teachers told me I was not paying attention. My IQ tests had shown I was bright, so they reasoned that I must not have been applying myself. It was so frustrating—I knew something was wrong, but I couldn't figure out why I was having so much trouble trying to read. (This has also since helped me to understand my own children's learning disabilities.)

Some years later I was told that my learning disability is called dyslexia. Kids nowadays who are diagnosed with dyslexia are helped and don't have to feel guilty about being unable to learn. But in Africa in the 1960s (and America, too, for that matter) youngsters with dyslexia were just told to put forth more effort.

The Tasok Boarding School was a time of growing

independence and self-reliance despite the loneliness and low self-esteem from my learning disorder. I had mastered ways to compensate for my lack of reading skills by finding other avenues for knowledge and assertion. I learned that I had a gift for drama and other creative pastimes. Although I was shy when I first came to Tasok, the fun and social activities helped me to fit in.

I still missed my parents terribly, but Ken and Dorothy, my dorm parents, were wonderful people who loved all the kids and went out of their way to help us through the difficult times. However, after that first year, they left the school and another couple took their place.

Uncle Joe and Aunt Min[1] were nothing like the loving couple that had preceded them. They seemed to resent their placement at the school and were gloomy most of the time. Sometimes they were even mean and abusive. I never recall either of them saying a kind or loving word to me. Uncle Joe seemed to believe that missionary kids should always be serious and never be the laughing, fun-loving, outgoing kids that we were. He often scolded me for "having too much personality" and being "frivolous."

I remember one night after dinner I was standing by the window looking out at the stars. We had study hall in the evenings and I was supposed to be doing my homework. But an unusual feeling of homesickness had

---

[1]Uncle Joe and Aunt Min are not their real names.

overwhelmed me and I went to the window to get a breath of fresh air.

Outside, it was already dark and I could hear the tree frogs chirping across the compound. I breathed in the moist fragrance of the tropical flowers growing outside and looked up at the stars that were already shining in the skies above the school. Without the "pollution" of city lights the stars were always a dazzling display against a black sky.

As I gazed at the stars a sudden thought came to me—*I wonder if Mother and Daddy can see the same stars that I see. And I wonder if they're looking at them now.* It was somehow reassuring to me to think that looking at the same stars might link us across the hundreds of miles that separated us.

Suddenly a man's scolding voice interrupted my reverie. "Why aren't you doing your homework?" Uncle Joe called out to me.

Instead of answering I asked, "Do you think that my mother and dad can see the same stars that I see? Wouldn't it be great if they could? Whenever I see the wishing star I wish I could see my parents."

"Young lady, I asked you why you weren't doing your homework. Answer me," commanded Uncle Joe.

"I have been doing my schoolwork," I told him. "But I got to feeling homesick so I went to the window to look for the wishing star. Then I began to think about my mother and dad and how much I miss—"

"Come here," he snapped, grabbing my arm and pulling me back to my chair. "If you can't keep busy with your homework, I'll give you another lesson. I don't ever want to catch you looking at those stars again when you're supposed to be doing your homework! Do you hear me? Your parents are missionaries, serving God. You're here to study and learn, not to mope around whining and thinking about your parents when you have work to do! Don't you know you'd be a great disappointment to your parents if they knew what you were doing? You're here to study; so forget about them!"

"You don't want me to think about my parents?" I asked him quizzically, positive that I had misunderstood him.

"You heard me! And to help you remember, I'm assigning you a five-hundred-word theme on why you should not be stargazing and wishing to go home. This is your home. Other kids don't mope and whine for their mommies and daddies!"

Uncle Joe told me that I had to write the theme and give it to him before I went to bed that night. When he left the room, I felt like crying. I couldn't think of a single word to write! How could I write on never wishing to see my folks again—such a thought was repugnant and a lie.

After an hour or two of nothing but a blank paper before me I decided that I had to write something, so I wrote what I thought he wanted me to say. It was *nearly midnight* when I finished—a terribly late hour for a small girl used to being in bed before nine o'clock. By the time that I completed those pages I was physically exhausted and emotionally wrung out.

I took the pages of the theme paper and walked down the hall to the dorm parents' apartment and knocked on the door. Uncle Joe was sitting at his desk waiting for me.

Blinking back tears, I handed the theme to him. He roughly took the pages from me and, without reading a word, ripped them in half, half again, then into smaller pieces—tearing them up into a handful of large confetti. Then he threw the pieces into my face and barked, "Let that be a lesson to you to not 'wish upon a star' to see your parents! I hope that this lesson will get that nonsense out of your system."

In later years I've concluded that he was probably trying to teach me that I had no "right" to miss my parents or to be homesick. In his warped sense of missionary self-sacrifice, he was punishing me for being too "selfish."

I ran back to my room crying and threw myself on my bed. I "flipped out" from the physical and emotional toll of the "lesson" and could not stop crying. I sobbed hysterically until I began to hyperventilate. When I had trouble breathing, I was frightened. My roommate panicked when she saw me curled up on the bed, rigid, sobbing loudly, and unable to breathe. She ran to get the dorm housemother, who called for Uncle Joe and Aunt Min to come.

I was still crying when they ordered me to stop and get control of myself, but I couldn't—so a doctor was called. When he came he sedated me and went across the room to talk in whispers with Uncle Joe.

My sister Amy was also called to come and try to calm me. That experience frightened her, and it became a bad time for both of us. Finally the sedative took over and I fell into a deep sleep.

The next day my parents were called and told that I was having an emotional breakdown and to come right away. My dad drove the mission car for the four-hour trip to the boarding school.

When Uncle Joe came to tell me that my father was coming to take me out of school for a few weeks to rest, he added, "If you tell anyone about what happened last night, things will be a lot harder for you when you come back to school!"

I was thoroughly afraid of him so I never told my dad, and neither Daddy nor Mother ever asked what caused me to break down. I never even confided in Amy what had happened until many years later.

On the four-hour trip back to my parents' home at the mission station I was quiet. Although they never asked me about the problem, I wondered if my parents had any idea of what it was like for me at the school.

For the couple of weeks that I rested at home, I was enormously happy. I followed my dad when he made hospital rounds and watched him as he cared for the sick and wounded. It was especially wonderful to go with him into the maternity ward where I saw all the newborn babies. I was even allowed to hold some of them. As I held these beautiful African babies in my arms, I was overcome with a strange feeling. There was something "right" about loving these babies and caring for them—as if I had discovered my calling. A seed of an idea began to grow in my mind—one day I'd open an orphanage in Africa and take care of all the unwanted children.

When I got back to school I decided to concentrate on my studies and not go out of my way to anger my dorm parents. Education was important to my father. He had made something of his own life by going to school—first to college, then seminary, and finally medical school. I was keenly conscious of not wanting to disappoint him in my own studies. However, I also felt confused and conflicted as I tried to fit in with the expectations of Uncle Joe and his wife. Although Uncle Joe never mentioned the incident that had triggered my having to go home, it was always an underlying part of our awkward and difficult relationship.

There was another episode involving Uncle Joe that is still vivid in my memory after all these years. During the school vacation my father had taken out my tonsils and adenoids at the mission hospital. An African assistant helped my father with the operation. When my father was done operating, the assistant finished by packing gauze into my nose and throat after surgery to help control the bleeding.

When the anesthesia wore off, the assistant took out the gauze packing. Unknown to him, when he had packed the gauze into my nasal cavities, the rubber tip of a small operating instrument fell into the material. However, when he took the packing out, the rubber tip stayed inside my nasal cavity, stuck in the back of my throat.

For the next eighteen months I was unable to breathe through my nose, was frequently sick, and no one knew why. It was often chalked up as the flu or some African "bug" that was hard to track down. I also developed bad, lingering halitosis caused by the rubber item (now unknowingly rotting inside of me).

It was my bad breath that caused the run-in with Uncle Joe that humiliated me and all but smothered what little self-esteem I had left. One day he came up to me and said bluntly, "You stink! Go brush your teeth."

"But I just *did*," I told him.

"Then do it again because you still stink."

My halitosis grew worse and I was sick more frequently. Finally the dorm parents called a doctor who, after examining me, called my dad, who came at once. When X-rays showed that a foreign object was lodged in my nasal cavity, he arranged to use the city hospital to remove it.

By now the object had petrified and was hard as rock. Tissue had grown around it and it was impossibly lodged. My father tried four different procedures to get it out, but in the end had to use surgery. The operation was painful, but not nearly as traumatic as the abusive words of Uncle Joe.

That distress was brought painfully to mind once again several years ago at a reunion of former missionary personnel who had served in Africa. Harold and I were in a buffet line when I caught sight of Uncle Joe and Aunt Min in line. Even after more than thirty years I shuddered with apprehension when I saw the couple. However, I tried to be friendly. "Hello," I said, "it's been many years since I've seen you. I don't think you've met my husband, Harold."

Looking down at my name tag to be sure he had recognized me, Uncle Joe said rather loudly, and with his usual bluntness, "We heard you got a divorce." I blushed with embarrassment.

Turning to Harold, Uncle Joe said, "Did she ever tell you how bad her breath was when she was a kid?"

Aunt Min added quickly, "Oh, she was so bad that nobody wanted to be near her!"

Back at our table, Harold (who knew nothing about the missionary couple) remarked to me, "Boy, those people are *weird!*" It was true. I hadn't seen them in some thirty-five years and Uncle Joe was still trying to assassinate my self-esteem. (I learned that they were still missionaries but had finally been transferred from the boarding school to an assignment where I hope they will do little damage to the lives of other children.)

God has truly helped me as I struggle with forgiving this couple for the anxiety and difficulty that I suffered while living under their care.

While Amy and I were at the Tasok Boarding School in Africa, my mother had homeschooled my younger sister and brother during their early years. I think that she became overly concerned about sending two more little children away to boarding school. Mother's stress took expression in severe asthma attacks. Meanwhile, my dad was often crippled by migraine headaches and was taking painkilling medications. In 1969 he decided to bring the family back to the United States where he went into private practice in Flushing, Michigan, and did part-time preaching.

Coming back to America during the height of the Vietnam War and protests was quite different for me. I was a high school student but could hardly remember my years in America. Africa seemed more like home to me. I missed being in the Congo (then called Zaire and since renamed the Republic of Congo).

My first day as a teenager in an American high school was a bit overwhelming. I wore an African muumuu dress, long and loose with no belt. I had no makeup or nylons and earned all kinds of stares from the other kids. There was no mistaking who the "missionary kid" was. I felt real peer pressure that day! I went back to school the next day but I had changed my appearance in order to "fit in" more with the other kids. I made a genuine effort to make new friends.

I had a flair for drama, music, and social activities and I guess that I *did* fit in—well enough to get a lead in school plays and run for homecoming queen. Yet I felt as though I was going through a "cultural identity crisis" because I really didn't feel that I belonged in America. When I protested the war in Vietnam I was out of step with a lot of traditionalists, even though my rebellion was more typically a part of growing up rather than political. For that reason, I didn't really fit in with the "hippie" crowd either.

There was no assurance of *belonging* to any group. I knew intellectually that I "belonged" to my family, but since I had spent my formative, "growing-up" years at a boarding school, I recalled that for much of my life it didn't seem that I belonged to my family. Also, since I didn't grow up with the other kids of Flushing High School, I didn't have much of a sense of belonging there either.

My heart and roots were in Africa and the only culture that I knew was in Africa—yet no one that I knew (aside from my family) understood that culture. I was growing homesick for Africa and my thoughts would often go back to the vision of that little missionary kid in her father's maternity ward, holding African babies and dreaming of one day running her own orphanage in Africa.

Although I did not realize it, God had been preparing me for my mission in life through these painful experiences. He knew that I would need to understand the feelings of abandonment, loneliness, fear, and the sense of not belonging—the same feelings that children from abusive, dysfunctional, and broken homes feel. But still more struggles awaited me as an adult.

CHAPTER TWO

Ricochet Romance

After graduation from high school I took a summer job at a resort hotel on the Atlantic seashore. The job had interesting ties to our family because my parents had also worked in the same hotel a generation earlier, when they were my age. It was hard work, but by way of it I was able to earn enough to start college in the fall.

During my senior year of high school I had dated a popular athlete who enlisted in the army after graduation. Stan[1] and I were quite infatuated with each other and our feelings grew in intensity while we were apart. I had gone off to my summer job as he went off to basic training camp. We wrote love letters back and forth for the summer and Stan came to see me for a week before he was sent to Germany. Our letters continued as I returned to the Midwest to attend Judson College in

---

[1]Not his real name

Elgin, Illinois (near Chicago).

At college registration I met a good-looking, outgoing older student named Steve. He became a friend and we started going out together while I continued to write love letters to Stan. This didn't seem at all unusual because my college friendship with Steve was just that—a friendship—in my mind. However, in the eyes of my friends and family, Steve was touted as the "one for me."

I thought about that with great seriousness. Stan and I still exchanged letters and he was oblivious that I was seeing another man. I truly felt that I was in love with Stan and that Steve and I were just good friends. Steve wanted to become more serious, but I wasn't sure. I wondered what to do.

My folks liked Steve. He was intelligent, personable as well as popular, and had clearly defined goals. He came from a good family—he was the son of a minister—and had a promising career.

Stan, on the other hand, didn't have the same family background. He was as bright as Steve and had been popular in high school. Yet, because he chose to enlist in the army instead of going to college I thought it would cause my folks to wonder if he really had serious goals and if he'd ever have a career as promising as Steve.

I felt a compelling need to please my family, so I evaluated the two men more with logic than emotion.

My heart had already been given to Stan and I had great love for him. Nevertheless, by putting down the pros and cons on a blank sheet of paper, Steve's list did look more promising. And by extension, my own life would be better if I married Steve. Ironically, I made my decision not purely on love or my own feelings but on what I thought my parents wanted. I chose Steve in order to please my parents and because I thought that it would make them proud of me.

We became engaged and we planned to get married in June. All during this period, though, I continued to write to Stan overseas. I couldn't bring myself to break up with him so I kept on writing. Several weeks before the scheduled wedding, however, I knew I had to tell him. In May I got up the courage to write him a "Dear John" letter. Meanwhile, Stan's mother had seen my engagement photo in the newspaper with a brief caption announcing a June wedding. She sent it to Stan. Her letter arrived about the same time that mine did.

Our wedding took place on June 1, 1974. Unknown to me at the time, Stan had gone to his base chaplain and asked for an emergency leave, and he was granted one. Stan thought that if he could see me and talk things over I'd change my mind. He flew back from Germany and arrived June 3, two days after the wedding—I was already on my honeymoon. Stan was devastated (as I learned sometime later).

As far as I was concerned, however, I had severed my ties with Stan. I looked forward to a lifetime of marriage to Steve accompanied by great happiness. Good intentions are never quite enough, though. At the time, Steve and I were both immature and selfish. It did not take long for the conflicts to start.

My mother had always placed my father on a pedestal and given him such allegiance that no one else in the world was as wonderful as he was. As a result I, too, had been convinced that Dad was perfect. How could anyone else ever measure up to those standards? To make matters worse, I not only compared Steve to my father, I judged him in comparison *to Stan*. He didn't stand a chance.

I did come to love Steve and we had some wonderful times—it wasn't all conflict.

We had two beautiful little girls—Jennie and Julie—within a few years. Jennie was always goal-oriented and logical. One day, when she was four-and-a-half-years old, I was giving her a bath after a day in Bible school. Jennie looked up at me with a serious expression on her little face. "Mommy," she said, "I want to ask Jesus into my heart."

"Really?" I said, smiling. "Do you know what that means, Jennie?"

She nodded soberly. "I think so," she answered. Just

to make sure, I explained what it meant and she understood. She prayed that night and asked Jesus to come into her heart.

Jennie was "Miss Responsibility" who made her bed before leaving for school and was always neat and organized. She dedicated her life to Christ in our church youth group and really became on fire for the Lord. She will graduate from Michigan State University with a four-year degree and plans to go on to nursing school, specializing in midwifery. She wants to become a missionary.

Our daughter Julie was not as highly organized and logical as her sister was, but she was a wonderfully talented and marvelous girl who always wanted to help people. Even as a toddler Julie demonstrated her sensitivity.

Julie has now successfully graduated from Avida School of Cosmetology and is working in Madison, Wisconsin.

Jennie and Julie both gave me such a sense of fulfillment and well-being as I poured myself into their lives to avoid focusing on my marriage to Steve and its failings.

Steve was a good father and provider, but our marriage was still pretty much a disaster. He was impulsive and had difficulty controlling his temper. On the other hand, I was demanding and difficult. Neither of us was walking with the Lord at the time and looking for His guidance.

I also looked for self-esteem outside the home. I worked in a hospital as a technician and later as a dental office manager. Both paid quite well and were rewarding in other ways as well. Yet I still felt empty and our marriage was in shambles.

Thinking that I could perhaps somehow find some spiritual strength for our marital struggles, I immersed myself in church work—helping in the Sunday school, singing in the choir, and leading the children's choir.

Then I came to the conclusion that I had never gotten over being in love with Stan—so Steve and I never had a chance. Steve and I paid a dear price for our mutual immaturity, anger, misplaced expectations, headstrong selfishness, and lies. As a result, nine years after getting married, Steve and I were divorced.

There was little acrimony between us when we separated. I expected a custody battle for keeping Jennie and Julie but Steve said, "I won't fight you on this. You're a good mother."

In the nine years that we were married, we had a lot of good times, but the divorce made us focus only on the bad times. Looking back, the marriage was doomed because I was foolishly comparing Steve against Stan and my father—and made virtually no effort to try to make the marriage work.

After the divorce I had a lot of growing up to do—

both emotionally *and spiritually*. Time helped to heal the emotional scars and hurts. Honesty with the Lord helped me grow spiritually. I first sought God's forgiveness in all that I had done to contribute to the failed marriage. I prayed for His guidance to help me be a good mother to my children and to release me from the anger, hurt, and guilt that the divorce had brought into my life.

During my own struggles I was also devastated to learn that my parents were having trouble with their own marriage—after thirty-eight years together. My father's migraine headaches had gotten worse after he left the African mission field. I didn't know this at the time, but in his battle to ease his headache pain, he prescribed himself painkilling medications. Soon he became addicted to them.

Back in America where he had started a private practice, his migraines still disabled him severely. He continued to use painkilling drugs and as a result his addiction grew worse. Finally another doctor friend intervened and told Dad he had to get help, which he did.

During that time, however, problems had developed in his marriage. My mother confronted him and they were divorced. Dad married his office nurse, who was much younger.

I unleashed my anger at Daddy and blamed him for destroying our wonderful family. I also resented my mother for always having placed my dad on a pedestal without acknowledging so much as a single flaw in his character. Yet I knew from my own failed marriage that there was probably plenty of blame to go around.

My own recovery was difficult enough. To watch my parents wrestle with the same issues and problems was almost worse. In a sense I felt that my father had betrayed me as well as my mother. It was terribly confusing and hurtful.

The struggles with my parents' divorcing gave me new insight into how my own divorce must have affected my daughters Jennie and Julie, and it grieved me terribly.

During this difficult and trying period I had sense enough to cry out to God and try to get right with Him. My prayers of repentance and pleas for forgiveness sustained me and gave me new courage as God gave me the peace and hope I needed to go on. There were constant promises from the Bible that also encouraged me and gave me guidance. I took strength from my quiet times with the Lord.

God helped me to take my focus away from my own feelings and actions and find ways of channeling my abilities toward helping others. From time to time a long-lost vision came back to me. It was a reminder of that adolescent girl on the mission field to someday return to start an orphanage in Africa.

It was as if God was reconfirming a call that He had given to me years before. Yet circumstances prevented me from going to Africa as a single mother of two young girls. So I continued working at the hospital while I prayed for the Lord to bring my calling for serving Him into sharper focus.

⌒

While I was going through the agonies of my divorce, there was a man experiencing his own marital difficulties. Harold Anglin, a soft-spoken high school biology teacher, had been struggling in his own marriage. He and his wife had four children—Jonathan, Jennifer, Amy, and Andrew. The couple had been separated for a long time but stayed married for the sake of the children.

When the older two children were grown, Harold and his wife divorced. She asked Harold for custody of the two children still at home and was granted it. However, a few months after the divorce became final, she changed her mind. Despite their differences, she had great respect for Harold's nurturing of the children and transferred custody of them to Harold.

Harold has always liked kids. Even as a youngster he took care of younger children and watched over other kids at play. In college he wasn't certain what he should do with his life. He had been a teacher's aide during college, helping out in the high school biology lab.

In the early 1960s he was encouraged to get his degree and become a professional teacher. A teaching job was thought to be opening up in the local high school when a longtime teacher announced his retirement. Harold asked for the position but the school was reluctant to make any changes until the older teacher left—keeping open the option that the teacher might change his mind and stay. In fact, the teacher *did* stay on past the end of school break in May, through June, July, and into August.

The teacher still had not resigned at the end of the school year so Harold's wife asked him to look for other, more secure work that he could begin right away, but Harold had faith that the job would open up. When the weeks stretched out into late summer, he still had no teaching contract for the fall and school was scheduled to start in two weeks.

Despite the fact that Harold held steady employment with a bookstore and had faith that the teaching job would open, his wife became increasingly anxious. But Harold asked her to have faith as he held out a while longer.

Two weeks before classes were to start, the retiring teacher finally gave his official notice. The school was ready then to replace him, and Harold applied for and got the position of high school biology teacher. He stayed in the same Michigan high school for thirty years, teaching biology, all but one of those years spent in the same classroom.

Harold thinks life is best when you "go with the flow" and don't fight your way against an impossible force you cannot overcome. One of his favorite stories from Civil War days illustrates the practical wisdom of "going with the flow." (Harold was born in the South and has a fondness for its history.)

He tells of some Tennessee soldiers who were ordered to cross a river that was swollen with the rains of several days. The water was high, the current was fast, and the river was extrawide at the crossing.

The strongest soldiers—and therefore the best swim-mers—decided on a direct course of action. They would swim across in a straight line to the other side. The others, not as confident of their swimming skills, decided on a different plan. They entered the water holding on to a large tree branch or floating log and let the current carry them along. They used their energy to steer the branch or log toward the opposite shore.

As it turned out, the swimmers who tried to make it in a straight line hadn't counted on the force of the current. They fought it all the way to the middle of the river, but the best that they achieved was a standstill position there. They were too exhausted to finish and couldn't go back. One by one they sank beneath the raging water and drowned.

The ones who let the current carry them got across — although they came ashore tired and cold a half-mile downriver — they survived — they made it across safely and that was all that mattered.

⁓

I met Harold horseback riding. He was a part-time deputy sheriff who worked some weekends as part of a horse patrol in a forest preserve. On this particular weekend Harold was on a trail ride with other friends from the mounted division. I was there riding horseback with a girlfriend when we met. As soon as he introduced himself and we had talked for a while I realized that I was interested. He was good-looking, muscular, a little shy but quite compelling, amusing, and a captivating conversationalist. As we talked Harold expressed himself with clarity and I found him fascinating. We were attracted to each other almost immediately. Harold asked me out and we soon began dating seriously.

We each learned that we had a great deal in common. The major area of agreement was in our love for our children. I learned that Harold had been the nurturer in his children's lives and continued to have an important role with them even after some had left home.

We became close friends, then fell deeply in love with one another. After a while we were married and blended our families. My daughters Jennie and Julie had a new stepfather and Harold's four children had a new stepmother. It wasn't always easy trying to make things go smoothly in the new household of eight persons, but we were committed to making it happen. We were also firmly committed to doing what was best, what was right, for our children.

Curiously, it wasn't until our son T. J. was born a year later that we were able to put these things into clearer focus. When it came to the child-rearing of T. J. we agreed on everything—feeding, discipline, toilet training, church, school, household rules, et cetera. It was only when it came to our *stepchildren* that we disagreed. When we finally saw that we were inconsistent toward each other's children we decided to establish common guidelines for all our children to keep them from being confused or frustrated.

My pregnancy with T. J. was unusually difficult. I suffered from a rare medical condition that permitted the baby in my womb to literally take all the minerals, body nutrients, and elements from my body and absorb them into its own. I nearly died before it was diagnosed. The treatment was extreme and had to be followed rigorously. When I was not hospitalized, I would visit the hospital several times a week for intravenous therapy. A bag of nutrient solution was hung and a drip needle was placed in my arm for "feeding." Each visit took four hours and I was forced to lie quietly while my body was refortified.

God used these periods of forced rest to renew my spiritual life as well as heal my body. I was reminded of the Bible verse, *Be still, and know that I am God* (Psalm 46:10). It was His peace, encouragement, and strength that enabled me to make it through that most difficult of pregnancies.

I had faith that God was allowing the baby to grow strong in my womb from the nutrients, vitamins, and minerals that he was taking from my body. However, there was no proof of that. What if I was simply losing these elements in body wastes and the baby was not benefiting? Yet, instead of worrying—about myself or the baby inside my womb—I relied on God's continuing promise: *Be still, and know that I am God.*

My doctors were concerned about the baby that I was carrying, though, and they were cautious right up to the time of his birth. When he was born, T. J. was not simply a normal healthy baby. He was *superhealthy* and made his appearance as a robust *ten-pound* baby boy. All those hospital IV treatments were forgotten as I gazed into his little face and wept tears of thanksgiving for the miracle that the Lord had performed in both our lives.

Just before his birth we had a family conference to discuss naming the baby that I was carrying. I knew by ultrasound tests that it would be a boy and asked the older children what they thought his name should be.

"Let's name him T. J.," suggested Julie. "I've always liked that name."

"Yeah, cool!" Andy exclaimed.

"You can't name a baby with initials!" my mother (who was helping me at the time) said. "The boy needs a *real* name."

"Then how about Travis?" someone offered.

"Travis is a strong Southern name," my husband, who comes from Alabama, remarked.

"No, I don't like that name," Mother answered. "It should be a more traditional-sounding name."

"How about Thomas James?" I suggested. "That way he could have a nickname of 'T. J.' Do you think that will work?"

That seemed to satisfy everyone. Several weeks later when the baby boy was born, he was greeted by the name T. J. and it stuck. Even my mother began calling him by his nickname when he was born.

When T. J. was two years old I was faced with yet another crisis. A rare, unknown virus attacked my left eye and caused a great swelling to the optic nerve. It was extremely painful and when I went to the doctor for help he was bewildered. Other doctors were consulted and they were just as mystified. The consensus was that perhaps it was an African virus, lying dormant for many years, but now was acting up.

The doctors were concerned, however, because the infection and swelling was in my optic nerve in the back of my eye, near the pituitary gland. In time it grew worse until I had total blindness in my one eye.

I adjusted as best I could to the loss of sight in my left eye, grateful that at least I could still see out of my right eye. But soon, the swelling made me also lose the sight in my good eye and *I was totally blind*.

In my darkness I recalled the lessons that God had taught me when I was pregnant with our son T. J. The Lord's promise applied just as well to my situation now—*Be still, and know that I am God.*

Harold and I prayed that God would heal me, but the damage appeared permanent and total. I resigned myself to a life of blindness and even signed up for a leader dog and sightless training. I had to learn how to cope with being blind and how to adjust to dealing with all of the everyday situations that I had always taken for granted.

Initially I tried to learn how to work in a kitchen—a place filled with dangers for someone who is blind. An occupational therapist came in to help me find my way around in my own home and learn how to find new ways to move through the house. All these were intended to help make my life a bit easier. The doctors prescribed massive doses of prednisone to attack the unknown virus but were otherwise stymied about how to treat me.

After being totally blind for six months I tried to resign myself to sightlessness for the rest of my life. One day I gave all my frustration to the Lord. I prayed, *Lord, I can do this if I have to because You've promised to give me all that I need. But I'd really appreciate it if You would give me back my sight. I suppose that I'm kind of selfish to ask You for such a miracle, but I want to see my baby's face again! I want to be able to serve You in some significant way. Please, Lord, will You answer my prayer?*

I never gave up hope and prayed daily for God to heal my eyes and bring back my sight—even though it was like asking for the miracle of being able to fly.

My months of darkness continued, as did my therapy in preparing to work with a leader dog and making all sorts of changes in our home to help me cope.

Then a miracle happened! Slowly, over several months, some vision returned. At first I could only sense changes in light. Then, as the weeks went by, I could also sense blurry movements in front of me. Finally, I was able to recognize the blurs as people. Then I saw faces and eventually could even read again.

Today my vision is almost perfect in my right eye. My left eye was left with some damage, but I am truly thankful to God that I can see as well as I do.

The doctors were less spiritual about my recovery. Although they could not identify the virus or tell me where it originated, they suddenly had all kinds of explanations as to how I recovered my sight. The one I liked the best was the practical observation of one doctor, who said, "Well, I suppose the best way to deal with a virus like this is to let it run its course." Perhaps, but I had chosen to give my predicament to God. I like what He can do with "impossible" situations.

The illness was serious and mysterious. God permitted it and used it as a means of making me rely more and more on Him.

Harold and I saw my blindness as a test of faith as well as a time to refocus our thoughts on truly important matters. I used the time to rededicate myself to whatever was first on God's list of priorities for my life.

It didn't take long for Him to reveal to us what He had in mind for us.

While T. J. was still a toddler a social worker came to our church and spoke about the growing need for foster parents. She painted a picture of the horrors of children without loving caretakers, growing up without affection and with all kinds of social and learning disorders.

I remember thinking how our evangelical churches were so outspoken and activist in the matter of opposing abortion, but ironically the church was silent on what should be done with the babies that *weren't* aborted.

Harold and I were stirred by the social worker's message. Later, at home, we prayed about becoming foster parents. By now several of our children were grown and away from home. We felt God telling us that there was room for other kids and we should help them by providing a loving Christian foster-care environment for them.

Harold and I decided to concentrate on special-needs children. When I baby-sat for special-needs kids a few years earlier God seemed to show me the importance of giving such babies lots of love and care. We began foster care by taking in newborn infants with special needs.

Many of these infants were born to underage moms in juvenile lockup. These babies were born addicted to crack cocaine or alcohol. Some had congenital physical impairments that might require a lifetime of special care.

We decided to care for special-needs infants during their initial month of life when parental rights were terminated by the court. Generally after that the babies would be placed for adoption. Sometimes adoptions took place quickly. Other times, especially in the case of real physical problems, placements were harder and adoptions took longer.

During those first few years that we were foster parents we cared for a number of babies and children. We lost count as to how many, but each one of them touched our hearts and lives in a special way.

Harold and I believed that our role as foster parents was a way to serve God as well as help a lot of special-needs children. But we had no idea of all that was in store for us as we began to follow that which we believed was God's calling for us.

Our older children were truly supportive of our calling to care for special-needs children. True, these youngsters were *our* ministry, but our biological children also were involved—and sometimes that involvement was not of their choosing. Many times they had to share their parents with our foster-care and adopted children, and because the special-needs kids needed so much more attention, I think they must have felt some loneliness, perhaps even alienation.

At first there was frustration and some resentment when they had a school function that Harold or I might not be able to attend because of a sick baby or other minor crisis. Yet, they all took it in stride and in the process each of them developed a sensitivity of their own for special-needs children.

Julie, at thirteen, looked for an assignment outside of the home and found a job as an aide in a public school classroom helping handicapped children. Julie loved this job and felt that being around kids and helping them was better than plain baby-sitting.

The teacher told me, "It's amazing to watch how this girl can reach out and help the little kids." There was a girl in a wheelchair who was much smaller than Julie because of her impairment, but they were the same age. Natalie was quite intelligent but shy and nonverbal.

One day Julie came home and told me about Natalie. "I can't believe how they dress her—like a little kid. And she's a teenager like me."

The next day Julie took a hair dryer, some rollers, and makeup to the school with her and, in her words, "dolled her up a bit." For several days after that the teacher noticed a difference in Natalie and told me about it. "I couldn't believe the difference! I've never seen Natalie so cheerful and happy." Julie had taken Natalie's pigtails out and brushed her hair, fixed her nails with clear polish, and put a little lipstick on her. Suddenly Natalie felt like all the other thirteen-year-old girls and her self-esteem soared.

Natalie looked forward to the times that Julie came to the classroom to help out. She helped Natalie on the computer and taught her to be more aware of things she could do without focusing on her impairments.

Once again the teacher went out of her way to tell me how pleased she was with Julie's contribution. "Julie has really changed this class," she said, adding, "She's even changed me as a teacher to become more sensitive to these special-needs kids. I was really proud of her."

Tragically, Natalie died of a respiratory infection before the end of the school year. Julie spoke at her memorial service. Natalie's mom came up to me at the conclusion of the service and said, "I can't tell you what a blessing your daughter has been in the life of our little Natalie this past year. The last year of her life was changed tremendously when Julie became her friend. Natalie was so happy."

Harold's children by his first marriage—John and Jennifer—were grown by the time we started the new family. His daughter Amy, his son Andy, and my two daughters, Jennie and Julie, still lived at home, but we felt that there was room for more.

This is when we opened our home to foster children. One of these children captured our hearts from the very beginning.

CHAPTER THREE

Brian's Song

Not all of the children in our foster care came to us as infants. There was one notable exception. His name was Pedro, a three-year-old Hispanic boy from a highly dysfunctional family. We did not know it at the time, but social workers had made elaborate plans to take all of the children out of the house in order to protect them from abusive and alcoholic parents. In a highly unusual move, a coordinated "raid" was staged at the house at *five o'clock in the morning*. This was done to make certain that the children would all be in one place asleep and not run off in the commotion of the raid.

We knew none of this background at the time. Our first contact came with a telephone call from a social worker asking if we would be foster parents for the three-year-old. Harold and I discussed the situation and agreed to take Pedro into our home.

The social worker seemed quite vague and unwilling to discuss the boy's background and tell us anything about him that would be helpful in helping him adjust to his new foster home. She simply told me in a hurried phone conversation, "I'll fill you in later. Can you take him right away, before the weekend?"

"Yes, I suppose so," I replied. "But can't you tell me anything about him? Can he talk? Does he understand English? Does he have any medical—"

"I'll tell you everything you need to know on Monday. I just wanted to make sure you could take him in right away. We'll be there within an hour," she said.

Our older children decided to give him a real Anglin "welcome" and made a huge banner to put up over the garage—*Welcome Pedro*.

We were all standing on the porch when the social worker's car pulled into the driveway an hour later. She got out of the car and looked a bit ruffled. Her hairdo was in disarray and her clothes were rumpled and the tail of her blouse was sticking out of her skirt. It looked as if she had been tussling with someone. Could it really have been the three-year-old?

That question was answered emphatically when the car door was opened and the social worker unbuckled the seat belt restraining the boy in the backseat. With unbridled energy the little boy tried to run away. He was screaming—not the nervous tears of a frightened three-year-old who had been forcibly taken from his home—rather, he was full of rage and fury, not at all afraid, just terribly angry.

The social worker grabbed him before he could get away and half-dragged him toward our front door. The boy was not going to cooperate. Pedro kicked the social worker's legs and bit her hand. He hammered her wildly in the stomach, all the while trying to wrench free from her grasp.

"Well, here he is," the social worked gasped. "Meet Pedro—but he goes by the nickname Pedi.[1] He's in your care now." With that she handed over the boy to Harold, who instinctively picked him up and held him close to prevent him from hitting or kicking anymore.

Pedi screamed and began crying out in Spanish.

"Does he understand any English?" I asked the social worker.

"Probably," she sighed. "I think that he knows English but he's never responded to anything I've said."

"B–but how will we get through to him?"

The social worker merely shrugged. "I'm sure you'll do fine," she said.

"But," I asked, "aren't you going to give us some background—?"

---

[1] Pronounced Pee-dee

She waved off my questions. "Listen, it was all I could do to get him here. He's yours now," the woman responded.

Three-year-old Pedi was drowning out our voices. He unleashed a torrent of swear words and kept it up as the social worker headed to her car.

I urgently ran after her. "But how do we get him to stop screaming? How will we know what he can eat? Does he have any allergies or anything?" I asked anxiously.

"I don't know, and frankly I'm too exhausted to be helpful with any advice. It was all I could do to get him here," she said, lifting her skirt to her knees to show me the bruises the three-year-old had inflicted. "Do whatever you have to do. He's your responsibility now. I'll call you on Monday to see how things are going." With that she drove away briskly down the street.

The next few hours were unforgettable. Harold had held Pedi close and kept him from hurting himself or others. For a long time Pedi screamed and thrust his tiny body in arching attempts to get away, but Harold's powerful arms were too strong. Harold walked for hours with the little boy in his arms. Finally, Pedi fell asleep and we put him to bed.

Recently I found an entry from my journal the day we took Pedi in. In reading it again I'm amazed that it can still bring such emotional feelings to the surface. But I'm even more amazed to see how concerned we were that day about Pedi and his entire family—the Lord seemed to blot out all the frustration of his arrival and helped us focus on just how awful it must have been for that family. Here's what I wrote that day:

July 6, 1988

It's been an exhausting day. With only a few hours to get ready for the arrival of a very angry and frightened little boy this morning, I find myself crying tonight. My heart goes out to Pedi's family, now torn apart. All eleven children were separated and put in different homes.

Those parents will have to go to sleep tonight not knowing where their children are or how they are doing. I can't imagine the guilt or loneliness that this family must be feeling. I wonder what caused such low self-esteem—or what happened to those parents as children themselves—to end up with such dysfunction that had them lose their entire family!

The only thing we know at this point is that Pedi's father was a drinker and very abusive physically and emotionally—to the mother as well as the children.

The social worker was pretty frustrated when she brought this little guy. From what she told us he kicked, slapped, and bit her on the way to our house. We had no idea what to expect! It didn't take us long—about one second after Pedi got out of the car—to discover that this little boy was like a wild child! Harold and I just looked at each other with bewilderment. I said, "Okay, Lord, this one is going to take some real patience."

I just went up a minute ago to check on the kids, who are all asleep now. Pedi is finally resting peacefully. He is so young and innocent. He is so confused about what is happening to him. Please, Lord, help me to help him. As I hold this child in the weeks to come, give me strength and guidance. Let this little child feel the love that we have to give and the comfort of our arms—just as You have always comforted me. But mostly, Lord, let me be an example to this precious little boy. Help me to not be judgmental about his parents but realize that they are also hurting and need forgiveness.

It's late now, and I'm really tired. I'm sure tomorrow will roll around before I know it!

Pedi was a little more restrained when he awoke that next

morning, but it wasn't long before he was trying to run away again. We took him to the kitchen and put him in a high chair that more or less constrained him. I poured some cereal into a bowl in front of him. Before I could put milk on it he grabbed the bowl with both hands and began stuffing the cereal into his mouth as fast as he could. It was as if he was afraid that someone else might take his food if he didn't eat it quickly enough.

I poured some more cereal into his bowl to reassure him that there was plenty to eat and he didn't have to worry. He looked at the bowl and then up at me with his big brown eyes and said, "How come you guys ain't got no bugs[1] in your cereal?"

On Monday we got the call from the social worker, who told us something of his background and why her department had been forced to act in the way it did to pick up all the children.

"How many children were there? Were there really eleven kids?" I asked.

"Yes. Eleven in all," she told me. "And they're all as wild as Pedi. I hope things are a little better today than they were when I dropped him off."

I chuckled. "Well, yes, things are better. Did you think that things could get worse?"

She laughed. "I'll be sending you his file—medical history, shots, stuff like that. I've got to tell you, this

---

[1] It took me a while to discover that he expected to find cockroaches in his food!

little boy has really been through a lot. There was terrible physical abuse going on in his biological family. There's even evidence of torture, and some of the children were burned with cigarettes!"

I had a sick feeling in the pit of my stomach as I listened to the social worker tell me about how this defenseless little boy had suffered so much. I think I must have blocked out much of the worst. Then I heard the social worker say, "Well, that's enough for now. I'll send you the file and check in with you later."

The months that followed were very trying. I had to constantly call upon God for His help. We had to deal with all kinds of physical and emotional problems that Pedi had acquired in his brief life in that dysfunctional family.

However, Pedi turned out to be a bright little boy. It didn't take him long at all to learn how to talk without using profanity. Once he was able to communicate some of his fears to us there was less frustration and anger.

But the night terrors continued for a long time. Harold and I would take turns reassuring him after he'd awaken from a terrible nightmare.

For the three years we had Pedi in our foster care he had adjusted quite well. Harold and I found ourselves facing another difficulty, though—one that came up too frequently.

In our role as foster parents we had taken in many little ones for various periods of time. Sometimes these foster children stayed only a short time, yet it was always long enough for us to bond with each one and learn to love them all. We kept a diary on each one and tried to make a difference in every little life before these children were placed in a different foster home or adopted.

It became a genuine traumatic event when they left our care to be placed in a different foster home, be returned to their birth mothers, or be adopted.

For us, the anguish of giving up these children that we had come to love was awful. When it was time for each of them to leave us there was a real time of grief and loss. We had come to love the children in our care and the anxiety of separation became a dark specter of gloom and emotional pain hanging over the prospect of their leaving.

The trauma of giving up these children after a few months—or worse, after several years—was terribly hard on both of us (as well as the children). Harold and I always grieved intensely when one of our foster children left us. The emotional pain caused by this separation finally got to be too much for us. One day Harold and I talked about it. "This is ridiculous," I told him. "Why should we constantly have to go through this process of grieving? Maybe we should consider adoption."

Harold agreed. "You're right—that's a good idea. It's awful when these kids leave our home. It's hard on all of us. We should adopt some of these kids and give them a permanent home."

As we discussed our idea we came to another area of agreement. We would adopt only "special-needs" kids —the ones no one else wanted. This was not some altruistic or glib decision on our part. It came after many years of deep personal struggles, preparation, and prayer.

After our decision was made we embarked on an exciting and miraculous adventure. We began to make plans to adopt Pedi, the little boy who came to us as a "wild child," and who was becoming a fully adjusted normal boy.

The Department of Children and Family Services had been unable to correct the problems in Pedi's biological home. The drinking and abuse could not be curbed, so the state put all of the children up for adoption. We had first option to adopt Pedi and we said yes.

There were occasional family visitations, and they were both touching and edgy for us. In the three years that we had been foster parents of Pedi, his mother had given birth to two more children!

I recall one time that Pedi's biological father came to see us. He seemed perplexed about all that had happened but saw no way for him to change things with the welfare people.

"Mrs. Anglin," he said softly, staring at the floor. "I have been trying to get custody of Pedi for a long time. I told the social worker that I wouldn't hurt him anymore. I really want to have my boy come back and live with us."

My heart ached at the sad state of affairs. Yet I knew that apart from all kinds of miracles, there was no way that he would ever be granted custody of his children. So did he.

"I know now that this is impossible," Pedi's father said sadly. "I know now that they will give Pedi to someone else to adopt."

I nodded, sharing in his sadness.

He continued. "I want you to know that if I cannot keep my boy, I want you to have him. I have seen how you care for him and love him. He is like one of your own. I hope that you will agree to adopt Pedi."

I assured him that I would and my eyes filled with tears at the feelings of great sorrow that I had for this man and his wife. I could not bring myself to harbor any bitterness or ill feelings toward them. They were victims, too.

I told Pedi's father that we would keep his family background and Hispanic heritage alive in Pedi's consciousness. I promised him that we'd never destroy his memories of his family, especially his brothers and sisters. We pledged to help him remember who he is and who his family was.

Although I was joyous at the prospect of not having to go through a custody hearing as part of the adoption process, I was deeply saddened and my heart ached for Pedi's mother and father. Whatever their failings, they still loved their little boy and would miss him greatly as the years passed and he would not see them again.

The process of adopting Pedi took over three years, and the adoption became final when Pedi was seven years old. As part of adopting him we allowed him to pick his own name. He chose a new name, *Brian,* and it became his own.

Brian has made remarkable progress since that day over a decade ago when that frightened, angry, and confused little boy came into our home.

Fast-forward nine years and look at Brian today. He is a tall, good-looking, highly intelligent student with a sensitive spirit, a wonderful personality, and a talent for creative writing.

In a school writing assignment, Brian and his brother, T. J., recently wrote an essay about their new baby brother, Zack (whom we will meet in a later chapter). Zack was born without fully developed arms and legs. Yet his limb deficiencies are not what his new brothers and sisters see. They see—but wait, I'll let Brian and T. J. tell you. This is what they wrote:

Perfection

There are different ways of looking at what perfection is. Some might say perfection is in an awesome sunset at the end of a fun-filled day.

Others might look at the magnificent Grand Canyon and determine there is nothing so perfect as it.

Yet others will look at the petals of a red rose and say, "Ah. . .this is perfection."

There is really no wrong concept as to what perfection is. It is in the eye of the beholder. For us, when we look at our new baby brother Zachary, born missing his lower arms and legs, we see perfection.

His smile is endearing, his laughter contagious, his eyes twinkle with joy.

Truly this is perfection in its purest form.

Harold and I had stepped out in faith when we said yes to the question of adopting special-needs children. God rewarded our faith and obedience to this calling by bringing into our home these little ones of such bright and beautiful potential.

As we look at Brian today we don't see a wild child— ignorant, angry, and bewildered. We see a creative, intelligent, sensitive, personable, and wonderful human being. It was all there inside him when he came to us that day. We only had to peel back the layers of hurt and resentment that he had built as a defense mechanism.

Brian is a life of unusual promise and we thank God for bringing him to us.

CHAPTER FOUR

Cierra—Our Ebony Angel

In mid-April 1990 I got a telephone call from a social worker. Knowing that Harold and I had a particular interest in and commitment to special-needs children, the social worker hoped that we might intervene in an unusual case.

I listened as she presented the case history. "She's an African-American child, thirteen years old, and she's in juvenile lockup for girls.

"She comes from several generations of drug addicts and prostitutes—each of these mothers gave birth to babies who were addicted to drugs.

"In this girl's case, her mother abandoned her in a crack house. By chance the grandmother got a phone call about midnight saying, 'Your daughter's baby is here and is pretty bad off. You better come and get it before it dies.' Well, the grandmother got up out of bed and drove all the way from Detroit to Flint to find the baby in the middle of the night. The baby was barely breathing when she got there and it was filthy. It hadn't eaten or been changed in a long time. She took her daughter's baby home and raised her—but the mother came back five years later and took the baby back.

"The child was raised for a time by her mother in terrible conditions. The mom neglected the child and we think that the mom's boyfriends abused the little girl—and who knows how many others who came and went might have abused her while the mother engaged in prostitution and drugs. So by the age of twelve this little girl was on the street herself. She got hooked on drugs and then prostitution."

"And you say that she's thirteen years old?" I asked.

"Yes," the social worker replied.

"Well, I'm sorry. I'm afraid she's a little too old for us. We've made it a policy not to take in any children who are older than the ones we already have. We think it is important for them to have some continuity and a sense of security," I added.

"Oh, I'm not talking about the thirteen-year-old girl," the social worker answered. "She's the *mother!* She's pregnant and will give birth in about two weeks! Then she'll be in lockup for up to a year after the birth.

We need a family that is experienced with special-needs children to care for this baby. It will be born addicted to crack cocaine and alcohol. Will you come and meet the girl and consider taking her in as a foster child?"

Harold and I discussed the circumstances and quickly agreed to check out the matter.

After meeting thirteen-year-old Iris[1] I had the unusual sense that we should be giving foster care to her—this young mother needed a mother every bit as much as the child she was carrying.

Iris and I seemed to strike an immediate friendship. After several visits I felt free to affirm her with lots of hugs and reassurances of our love for her and her baby. I also looked for opportunities to let her know about God's love for her and her baby.

I had watched her situation at the lockup as she interacted with the supervisory staff. They seldom made human contact with those in their charge. There were at least a few who would have questioned my reaching out to Iris with the kind of unconditional love that Jesus showed when He went to sinful and unloving people. He set the example; we are told to model His love.

"Besides," I told one of the supervisors, "how can you be angry at a thirteen-year-old girl for the bad choices she made that did so much harm to her unborn baby?"

Iris and I talked about her life, her dysfunctional

---

[1]Not her real name

family, and her baby. Then I asked her what she wanted for her child.

She sat back in the chair and looked past me while she thought about my question. Then she replied, "Miz Anglin, more than ever I want my baby to have a good home. I don't want her to make the same mistakes I made—and my momma made. I ain't sure that I can be a good momma to my baby."

I visited Iris every day while she waited to give birth. On May 1, the day of delivery, she wanted me to be with her in the hospital room. When the baby was born the nurse held up a tiny, fragile infant.

"Look, Iris," the nurse said as she washed the baby and wrapped it in a small blanket, "It's a girl. Don't you want to hold her?"

Iris shook her head and told the nurse, "No. Give her to Miz Anglin. She knows how to hold a baby and take care of it. I'm afraid I'd drop her or somethin'."

I took the small baby and held her close to my breast. The infant made no cry but shook violently from the tremors of cocaine withdrawal—too weak to move her arms or legs. After a moment or so I walked over to Iris's bed and placed the baby beside her.

Stepping back, I watched as one child gazed at another. A little girl was looking at her own baby in a scene that looked as if she were playing with a lifelike doll. My heart felt the same ache that I had experienced when I first met Iris—an anguish that would haunt me for years to come. Both of these children needed a mother to love them and care for them. But I was able to help only the most helpless one. How I wished that there would have been a way for me to take them both in. At this instant an idea was planted in my subconscious mind that would only be revealed to me years later as a concept developed for a halfway house where young girls could come and learn how to be mothers to their babies. But more about that later.

"Have you thought of a name for your baby?" I asked Iris.

"Yes, Miz Anglin, I have. Do you like the name Cierra—spelled with a 'C'?" she asked.

"I do like it, Iris. Cierra is a beautiful name. And she's a gorgeous baby. You've made a good choice." I smiled in agreement with her selection of the name.

"Miz Anglin," Iris said as I was getting ready to leave the hospital and drive home, "I'm really glad you're gonna take care of Cierra. I like you a lot and I know you're gonna be real nice to her."

I smiled and bent down to kiss her forehead. "Good night, Iris. I'll be praying for you and I'll be back to see you," I told her.

Cierra was kept in the neonatal intensive care unit so

that the hospital personnel could monitor the baby's withdrawal from drugs and make sure that she kept breathing. That night at home I wrote a letter to the tiny baby still in the hospital. It was the first entry in her personal life journal:

Dear Cierra,

What a beautiful baby you are!—six pounds and seven ounces and twenty-one inches long. You are a precious package from heaven. Today is your beginning and you have so many new life experiences to come. I pray that they will be positive and that you will meet each challenge that God gives you with your head held high.

Look to Him for your strength and guidance and you will grow into a beautiful young woman.

You are a very special little girl, Cierra. Today when I held you for the first time I thought about how lucky I was to have the opportunity to be a part of your life. I pray that God will hold you in the palm of His hand and that He will help me as we begin our journey together.

This is your life journal, Cierra. All the words that I write come from my heart. I love you, sweet baby!

Iris stayed in the hospital only one day and had to be returned to the juvenile lockup. However, she was permitted to come back to visit the hospital and see Cierra, still on monitoring equipment. Her brief few visits to see her daughter were tentative and unsure. She did not know how to relate to the fragile life in the incubator crib. The nurses were perhaps a little more cynical than I was. One suggested that Iris would probably not even come to see the baby if the state hadn't offered her a chance to get out of lockup for a few hours.

I came every day to visit Cierra and was usually there when Iris came. I showed Iris how to hold her baby and talked to her about making a change in her life by giving it over to God. She was open to the idea and I could tell that she wanted to change but wasn't quite sure she wanted to give up drinking, drugs, and sex— those things that had gotten this thirteen-year-old into trouble in the first place.

It was obvious to me that Iris loved Cierra, as best she could with so little understanding of what a mother's love is. During the hospital visits I found that in modeling what maternal love was like I became a "mother" to both Cierra and *her* mother, thirteen-year-old Iris.

When Cierra was released from the hospital I took her home. She still had traces of drugs and alcohol in her tiny, fragile body and she faced more of the harsh symptoms of withdrawal. The tremors had eased somewhat but her little body would still frequently go rigid and her small muscles would tense. Cierra was constantly restless and hardly slept well at all.

For nearly four months we had many difficult nights when Cierra couldn't sleep. The older children helped me by holding and rocking her during the day when she was restless. Harold and I took turns walking the floor with her at night. Her life journal entries tell something of her early struggles.

May 28, 1990
Dear Cierra,

Today you are resting peacefully after a very difficult night. We both need to sleep for about two days! You began crying last night at eight o'clock after being restless all day. From eight P.M. until four A.M. you cried off and on—mostly on!

It's hard to know how to comfort you. Sometimes nothing seems to work. Mostly I hold you gently and whisper that we love you. I have faith that one day you'll respond to us and your little tense body will relax.

You are loved so much, Cierra! Tomorrow we will visit the doctor. Daddy will be going with us. Usually you like the car ride so maybe the trip will be a quiet one.

I want you to know how good the other children are with you. They understand your problems and have patience with you. Julie has walked the floor with you many times and even little T. J. tries to comfort you. I pray that your distress will not last too long.

In June my mother visited us from Florida. It was the first time she had visited since Cierra was born. Although the baby was still crying and restless, Mother held her and fell in love with Cierra from the first moment.

As I watched Mother holding little Cierra, I recalled how she had been as a mother to me—so patient and loving. She was my own model for motherhood since she was the sweetest, kindest Christian that I knew. Mother never raised her voice and always had a gentle touch.

My eyes filled with tears of joy as I thought about the great gift that God had given me in my own mother. It hurt me to think that Iris and her mother never had that wonderful connection, nor was Iris able to model what a mother is to her little baby. She was hardly much older than Cierra herself.

In my journal letter to Cierra that day in June, I told her that I had often thought of my mother as an angel in disguise and have tried to pattern myself after her.

Mother rocked Cierra in the rocking chair and sang softly to her. Despite the problems that existed for both Iris and Cierra, I prayed for them. I especially prayed for the little baby that Mother was holding—and asked God that the dysfunction that was generations in the making might be broken and that Cierra might overcome all the negative and destructive elements that had been so much a part of her life until now.

> *Cierra, I pray that God will give you the same kind of beautiful, happy childhood that I had.*

As Cierra continued to fight the tremors and effects of the drugs in her system, it seemed that we would win one skirmish only to encounter another.

Three different times Cierra stopped breathing as I held her. Panic-stricken, I laid her down and began giving her mouth-to-mouth resuscitation. Thankfully she began to breathe again each time that I breathed into her. But I was scared to think of what might happen if she stopped breathing in the night or when I wasn't holding her.

I called the pediatrician for advice. I was told that a device had been developed that would monitor Cierra's breathing. If for any reason she stopped breathing, an alarm would sound to wake me so that I could help her. The monitor needed to be attached to Cierra twenty-four hours a day. But it gave us all a greater sense of security and peace of mind.

July 15, 1990

Dear Cierra,

Today has been a rough one. You are sleeping peacefully now and I pray that you will stay calm through the night. You have been having trouble with your breathing at night so the doctor has put you on a breathing monitor around the clock. We have to put two patches on each side of your chest under your arms. Wires are attached to the patches that lead to the portable machine. You must stay on it at all times. The doctor is afraid that you might stop breathing when you go to sleep. So, for a while your machine will be a part of our daily living.

I am so thankful that there are machines now to use as a precaution because your life is important and we will do everything possible to ensure that it is long.

I worry that you will scare your mother when you go to visit her. Somehow we'll have to make sure she understands that your machine should make her feel more comfortable, not scared.

Sleep tight, my sweetheart. I'm tired, but I know I will sleep better knowing that if you do have trouble in the night the alarm on your machine will wake me up to help you.

Night, night.

Cierra was born with a low birth weight (actually in the lowest twenty-five percent category) but in her time with us had improved dramatically so that her current weight was in the fifty percent range. Likewise, her head circumference was in the lowest ten percent range at birth but after nine months with us she began to grow normally.

Agency records at the time reported, "While in the Anglins' care from age 0–8 months, Cierra's head circumference, weight, length all steadily progressed."

Everyone seemed pleased with the remarkable improvements being made in the baby's life despite the terrible initial setback from the effects of alcohol and crack cocaine addictions of the mother.

Somehow we all managed to get through those difficult days of the first nine months of Cierra's early life. One thing troubled me more than anything else did, however. The social workers that provided oversight for Cierra had indicated that parental rights would be terminated for now-fourteen-year-old Iris, Cierra's biological mother. That would open the door for us to adopt her. But we were troubled by the fact that both Harold and I were so bonded with Cierra that we feared any complications for the next step—the adoption. Until the process is final all kinds of things can go wrong.

I had secretly been afraid that something might happen to make it impossible to adopt her. There are a lot of home studies, various reports, investigations, and paperwork to be done. Even then, there's always the possibility that the mother could appeal the decision and tie the matter up in court for many months—or even a year or more.

Although we had been reassured by Cierra's social workers that everything was working in our favor, Iris's caseworker was an altogether different person and gave no indication of his thoughts about the case.

To be a bit more certain of the steps ahead, I approached the subject with Iris, asking what she thought about our adopting Cierra when parental rights were terminated. In her eyes was a mixture of sadness and relief, almost as I had expected.

"Miz Anglin," Iris said softly and thoughtfully, "I know I'll have to give her up. I ain't really old enough or practiced enough to be a real momma. But if I *do* have to give her up, I want you and Mr. Anglin to have her. I know that you love her and that you'll always take real good care of her."

The social workers encouraged us as well. There was no way that Iris would change her mind. She couldn't keep the baby and hadn't anyone else that she trusted to take Cierra. Thus reassured, Harold and I made known to Iris's social worker our tremendous desire to adopt Cierra.

For this reason I suppose a lot of foster parents and prospective adoptive parents are most vulnerable in terms of their feelings. With the prospect of becoming a parent to the little one you are caring for, the parents— especially the foster mother—put all their emotional energy into the child. Yet, with even a remote possibility of having the child taken away from them, there is the tendency to not invest the totality of their emotions—to hold back something of themselves so as to not be hurt if the unthinkable were to happen.

I've always suspected that a child knows intuitively when she is a permanent part of a family. Likewise I wonder if she can also know if a foster parent is holding back some of her emotional attachment out of fear of eventual separation. I decided to give all of my emotional energy, unconditionally, no matter what happened with Cierra's adoption.

The social worker that was Cierra's caseworker had reassured us that the road was clear for our adoption. The state had already decreed that Iris was not qualified to be a parent and had already started the process of terminating her parental rights, which Iris had accepted without too much difficulty.

However, Iris's caseworker seemed to distance himself from us when we told him about our wishes to adopt Cierra. Immediately we sensed some resistance to our plans. He made no secret of the fact that he didn't approve of what we wanted to do.

"I don't believe in cross-racial placements," he said simply. "I think they are wrong, and I won't approve it."

"But isn't it against the law or regulations to discriminate like that?" I asked him, knowing full well that it *was* the law not to discriminate.

"Yes, uh, technically it is," he replied.

"You mean that you're going to deny our adoption because you don't believe in cross-racial adoptions?"

"Oh, I didn't say that. I just think it's better to give the biological mother a chance to raise her own baby. If I need to, I can find other reasons to deny the adoption."

He probably *could* find a legal reason to deny our petition to adopt Cierra, but we both knew the real reason. I felt sick. No matter how noble the idea of having a biological mother raise her own child, it was never going to work, and we both knew it. For whatever reasons, on his own agenda he was simply buying more time.

"Please, don't do this," I pleaded with him. "We love this little baby. We've bonded with her. She's begun to overcome the problems of her birth and is growing in wonderful ways. If you take her from us now you will undo all that good. She will suffer even more harm than she already has! You know that the experts say that there's a risk of a lifetime of emotional problems and attachment disorder if a child is taken away after bonding. Cierra's made a terrific attachment with us and with our family. Putting her in different foster homes until you find some other foster parents or another couple is not in her best interests. Why would you even consider it? Please don't change things now."

But the social worker was insistent. He decided that Iris and Cierra should be placed in a foster home *together*. That way, he reasoned, Iris could be supervised as she took care of her baby.

"You already know that isn't going to work," I said, probably a little too bluntly. My feelings were churning inside.

"The other social workers have said that giving the baby to Iris would be a great disaster for both of them," I added, looking for any rational idea to keep him from implementing his plan.

"It *will* work," he said stubbornly. "I'm going to petition that Iris and the baby be placed in foster care together where she can raise Cierra in a supervised environment."

"Then let them both stay at *our* house. We'll be foster parents for the two of them," I countered.

"No," he said quickly. "I think it's best for you and your husband to not have anything to do with Cierra or Iris. There would be too much confusion for the baby. Cierra won't bond to Iris as long as you and your husband are in the picture."

I bit my tongue to keep from responding along the lines of my feelings. Taking a deep breath I softened my voice and asked, "But can we visit them?" I was running out of hope.

"No. I told you; it's too confusing and disrupting. You will have no more contact with the baby after tomorrow."

"Tomorrow!" I cried. "You want to take her tomorrow? Why so soon?"

"It's just best that way," the social worker answered vaguely.

"But at least let us be able to visit Iris and Cierra. There are so many things that Iris doesn't know about her baby—how to use the breathing monitor, how to handle her seizures, what she eats, what she's allergic to. Please—at least let us visit regularly," I all but begged.

"There'll be less of a risk of attachment disorder if we're allowed frequent visits," I continued. "We can provide continuity until Iris and Cierra are fully bonded. It will prevent Cierra from having a feeling that Harold and I have totally abandoned her," I explained.

"All right," the social worker said with a sigh of resignation. "You can visit them whenever you want. I'll work out the details tomorrow when we take the baby."

By the time I got home and told the family the tragic news we were all in a state of deep anguish. This separation trauma was the reason that Harold and I had decided to *adopt* rather than be simply foster parents.

We had been given all kinds of assurances that we'd be able to move forward with Cierra's adoption. It hadn't occurred to us that we'd be denied on what seemed to us racist considerations.

Our older children took the news badly. They loved little Cierra and cried when they heard we had to let her go. They all took turns holding her that night, each one telling Cierra how much he or she loved her and each sharing something special that he or she would remember about her.

Later that night, I stood looking out the window. It was the middle of January and very cold, dark, and bleak. It matched the mood of my soul. I tried very hard not to cry in front of the children, but now they were all asleep. Harold was holding Cierra in his comfortable chair and whispering songs as he rocked her.

As I looked at the two of them in the other room, deep feelings of love for Harold and Cierra overwhelmed me. I couldn't hold back my tears any longer. Turning away, I muffled my sobs in my hands. Sometime before midnight I wrote what I thought might be a last letter to Cierra.

January 17, 1991
My Sweet Baby Cierra,

Tomorrow I must say good-bye to you for a time. You will be leaving with your mother. It is right for you to have a chance with your mother. She loves you and wants to make things work, but I am so worried that you will feel that Daddy and I abandoned you.

I am so disappointed in the people I trusted. You see, sweetheart, what we planned (and agreed to in our meeting with the social workers last Monday) is now going to change. You will be leaving tomorrow afternoon. They promised you would come back and visit and that we could visit you, as often as we wanted, but in my soul I am afraid that when you leave my arms tomorrow they will change their minds.

I pray that my fears do not come true. There will be so many things for you to get used to.

Cierra, we love you so much; my heart is hurting so. We have had so many children come and go. All have touched our hearts but only a few have woven themselves into the very fabric of our being. You, Cierra, are one of those children.

Before you went to sleep tonight we had a celebration of the time you have been with us. Each child held you and told you how much you meant to them. We sang songs, we laughed, and we cried together. It's very hard for the children to think of you as leaving. They all think of you as their baby sister and they will miss you deeply.

As for Daddy, well, I can only say that he has spent much time planning and dreaming about you. At this very moment he is holding you in his arms while you sleep and he is whispering some songs to you. . . . I have no doubt that he will hold you 'til morning's light. Then he will be strong for the children and me, but then he will go into his woods where he will cry and grieve your leaving.

My mind drifted and my thoughts left the page long enough to reflect upon Cierra's time with us. I prayed that God would go with this tiny baby girl when she left our care—asking Him to protect and help her.

It is interesting to me that as I reflected over the past nine months that Cierra had been with us I never once thought of the problems, only of the joy. For those wonderful months she had enriched our lives as we tried to nurture and love her.

However, I shuddered as I thought of the possible devastation that might come into her little life after tomorrow.

The next day all my worst fears came true. We were told that guardianship had suddenly been transferred from the agency that we were working with and given to Iris's caseworker's agency.

When I asked the caseworker for details about where Iris and Cierra were going and about visitation, the caseworker told me, "But I told you yesterday that I think it's in the best interest of the mother and baby that you no longer be a part of their lives. It's too confusing," he said.

"Yes, and then you said you would allow us to visit them to help prevent feelings of abandonment and to ease the transition," I reminded him.

"No, you misunderstood. I didn't say that."

He looked at me directly and we both knew he was lying. He had said those things just to get rid of me. I knew then that the caseworker would never tell us where they were taking them.

Suddenly it was time to transfer the baby to the agency. It was as if Cierra was being ripped from my arms, taken from the only parents that she knew and spirited somewhere else, never to see us again.

The next few days were a nightmare. It was agonizing to walk into Cierra's bedroom and see her empty bed. I cried much of the time and called out to God in prayers that were not much more than fragments of desperate longing.

After a week or so of worrying and wondering, I thought about "bucking the system" to try to regain the promised visitation rights. Ordinarily I am not a disruptive person but I felt an injustice was being done.

"This baby can't speak for herself," I told Harold. "I'm going to have to speak for her."

Harold and I both knew that there were risks inherent in "making waves." While many social workers would understand our concern and let us state our case, we knew that Iris's caseworker would resent our efforts as simply efforts to try to overturn his decisions. He could even create problems for us in trying to be foster parents or adoptive parents in the future.

I decided not to be intimidated by that possibility. The foster-care network is one I knew quite well so I started to make some phone calls to see if I could find out anything about where the caseworker had taken Iris and Cierra. I also called other social workers that we knew, as well as contacts in various baby placement agencies.

"I'm sorry, Mrs. Anglin," one state agency social worker told me, "but our hands are tied. Once the guardianship went from the baby's agency to the mother's agency, we lost any authority in the matter."

"But what about the baby?" I cried. "Isn't there anyone who's supposed to look after the rights of the baby?"

"Well, I know that *you* care about the baby. Keep trying to find a sympathetic ear," the social worker said. "You're getting close. Calling your network will help. I can't tell you where they are, but I can tell you they aren't in Detroit."

"I thought they'd be in Detroit because that's where Iris lives, and so does her family," I told her.

"Yes, but they're somewhere else, not Detroit. That's all I can say."

That was critical information. It would be a lot easier to track them down after eliminating Detroit.

I thought it might be best to try one last time in

changing the mind of the caseworker that took Cierra. When he picked up the phone and learned who was calling, I could sense contempt and condescension in his voice. "Now what is it, Mrs. Anglin?"

"I know we had an understanding the day before we gave up Cierra and I know you probably felt it was easier to promise me that I could visit Cierra than to argue with me. I understand that. But in the interest of the baby, I'm asking you to reconsider," I asked.

"No," was his simple, curt reply. "Is that all?"

"No, sir, it is not," I answered, doing my best to maintain a polite and civil tone. "I want you to know that I can be your best friend or your worst nightmare. I'm an advocate for Cierra. That baby can't speak for herself, and I disagree with you that you're acting in her best interests. You say we're a team—social workers, foster parents, and adoption agencies. But you don't trust us. Foster parents are good enough to care for the baby, nurture the baby, and do all things for the baby. But when it's time to *speak* for the baby, you tell us to forget it—that we have no say in the matter. We're not important in such matters. But that's wrong! I have much more invested in this child than you do—more than *any* social worker in the system. I know this child; you only know her as a case number and file.

"You don't even know what she looks like. Tell me,

what color are her eyes? How tall is she? How much does she weigh? You should know—that's all in her file. But you don't know. Nor do you know the funny things she can do, her favorite toys, the songs she likes, or how she acts when she's hungry or tired. You don't know any of these things, do you?"

"Mrs. Anglin," he sighed. "I can live with myself over this. And you know why? It's because I make decisions based on logic and not emotion. You're too close to her. I know that you've had her since birth. I also know that the files tell me what a wonderful job you and your husband have done as foster parents. That's commendable. But you are no longer caring for this child. You've got to give it up!"

"Excuse me, sir!" I said sharply. "I'll never give up on her, not as long as I have breath still in me!" Then I hung up.

CHAPTER FIVE

Reunion

I spent the next three months looking for Iris and Cierra. Every day I called people in my network of foster-care parents to see if they knew anything.

Finally, after scores of phone calls, I learned that Iris and Cierra were in a foster home in Flint. After a few more days and more telephone calls I even learned the name and address for that home.

Looking up the name in the Flint telephone directory, I dialed the number. I was surprised to hear a familiar voice answer the phone.

"Iris?" I asked. "Is that you? This is Patty Anglin."

"Oh, Miz Anglin," Iris squealed, "I'm so glad to hear from you!"

We talked for several minutes and I mentioned that I was surprised to hear her answer the phone instead of the foster parent.

"Well, she teaches school," Iris said, "so she ain't here during the daytime. She'll be comin' home about four-thirty."

"Are you there by yourself all day?" I asked.

"Oh, no. Cierra is with me," Iris answered.

"Iris, would you mind if I came to visit you and Cierra?"

"Oh, I'd like that very much, Miz Anglin," Iris replied.

I called back later and talked to the foster mother and told her that Iris had given her okay to a visit. She warmly invited me to come.

Before visiting Iris and Cierra I took out the photos that I had taken the day that Cierra was taken from us. She looked bright and cheerful. Her beautiful eyes were expressive and seemed like wonderful portals into her personality and a reflection of her soul. My own eyes filled with tears at the joyous prospect of seeing her again.

I drove up to the modest home and rang the doorbell. The foster mother was at home and after I introduced myself she welcomed me inside.

Iris came from another room when she heard the doorbell. When we saw each other we embraced and Iris told me that she had missed me.

"I didn't think we'd ever see each other again," she said. "They told me that you weren't coming around anymore."

"Where's Cierra?" I asked after a few minutes of conversation with Iris.

"She's in our room—I'll go get her. She's getting so big and wants to crawl all over so I have to keep her in the crib most of the time. I don't have a playpen," Iris said.

When she came back into the room with the baby my stomach churned. I tried not to appear shocked, but I was appalled at the change that had taken place in Cierra.

I was expecting to see the bright, cheerful, and happy child of the photos I had looked at the night before. Instead, her small, round face was blank. Her eyes were dull and listless. She showed absolutely no recognition when I held out my arms to hold her. In fact, she was shy and withdrawn and acted a little afraid of me.

I nearly burst into tears but bit my lip as I took her into my arms. I held her close to my chest, hoping that she'd remember my heartbeat. For half an hour I sang familiar songs to her and whispered loving words into her ear.

It broke my heart that all attachment seemed to be broken, and my spirit was heavy with grief.

When it was time for me to go, I felt that there was

at least a small glimmer of recognition from Cierra, but she was an altogether different person.

When Iris picked her up and took her back to their room, the foster mom said to me privately, "I don't think the baby is doing very well. I try to help Iris, but she doesn't have a clue about being a mom. I teach school, so I'm gone during the day and she's on her own.

"Sometimes when I get home, I have to scold Iris because the baby hasn't been changed in a long time. Or maybe she forgot to feed her. If you ask me, she's too young to be a mother.

"I can't watch her all the time. I'm supposed to monitor her to make sure that there isn't any abuse, but I can't teach her every little thing about taking care of a baby."

I listened but said nothing. The woman continued, "You can't expect her to take care of a baby—she's just a kid herself. But she can't even take care of herself. Three weeks after they released her from the juvenile lockup, she got pregnant again."

I left quickly and by the time I got to my car the tears came in a flood. All kinds of feelings were released—anger, resentment, sorrow, love, and compassion—and I was troubled all the way home.

Iris had asked Harold and me to come back for other visits and we did come as often as we could. Each time I'd show Iris some skills of baby care. I reminded her how important it was to spend time with the baby and not just leave her in the crib.

"Cierra doesn't cry like other babies so you won't always know when she's hungry or needs to be changed. You'll have to check up on her all the time. You'll have to get to know her schedule and needs," I said.

I felt sorry for Iris. I knew that it wasn't her fault that this experiment was such a failure. She was too young and too immature to know what to be doing. Not only that, Cierra had so many other needs. You couldn't expect a fourteen-year-old to know how to deal with allergies, asthma, various therapies, and the other problems of Cierra's brief lifetime.

Addicted babies are shown to be more susceptible to all kinds of neurological disorders, have Attention Deficit Disorder, learning disabilities, developmental delays, hypersensitivity, irritability, poor impulse controls, easy distractibility, low frustration level, be less goal-directed, language difficulties, less of a feeling of security, and trouble with attachment. Addicted babies often are plagued with respiratory and kidney trouble, visual problems, delays in motor skills, malformation of body organs and the spinal column, an increased risk of strokes and seizures, and they usually have lower IQ levels than other children their age. Such a list would be intimidating to nearly any mother.

I couldn't imagine what would happen if, suddenly, Cierra had one of her asthma attacks. Her young mother would have panicked, not knowing what to do—even though these were things the agencies tried to address with her. But she had no skills with which to address them. Fourteen-year-old Iris would have trouble coping with a fully normal child.

No, I really couldn't blame Iris. The system, in effect, sacrifices children for "mothers' rights." Everyone says that children have rights, but when there is a contest the mother's rights usually overrule the child's rights. My complaint is that the children have no one to speak for them in these debates.

I couldn't fault the foster mom, either. The system knew when Iris and Cierra were placed in that home that the foster mother was a schoolteacher and wasn't available full-time to monitor the teenager and her baby. Not only that, I knew Iris was easily swayed by her peers. If she was alone during the day, it was more than likely that boyfriends and girlfriends came over to see her and that was the situation that had caused all sorts of trouble in the past.

I made a few telephone calls to friends in the social services agency to report what I saw. As dispassionately as I could I listed my observations.

The woman on the phone listened, then told me,

"You're right. Our caseworkers have been out to check on Cierra and Iris and their reports tell a pretty bleak story.

"Listen to this report: 'Cierra continues to show clear signs of being exposed to alcohol and crack *in utero* during the first and possibly second trimesters of gestation.' Then it goes on to tell how she was at the lower percentiles in just about every area when she was born. Then it says, 'She has exhibited irritability to the point of inconsolability, an exaggerated startle reflex, accompanied by an arching of the back and flailing of the limbs' and so forth."

"She never did that before," I mentioned.

"No, when Cierra was with you she was thriving despite her problems. But now she's regressing. And this is what's on her chart now."

"What does it mean?" I asked.

"Well. . ." The woman seemed reluctant to talk about it.

"Please; I need to know," I pleaded.

"From that exaggerated startle reflex and the arching of her back behavior we suspect possible physical abuse. Maybe from a boyfriend. Probably not Iris, but we don't know for sure. And there's a large bruise on her back that nobody can explain," the social worker said sadly.

I wept silently as I held the telephone and listened to

the horrors being read so matter-of-factly from the report. Finally, I groaned loudly and asked, "Can't you do anything? Do we have to wait until the baby dies?"

"I know, Patty," she answered. "We're on it. We're going to take care of it."

I sighed with relief. Over the past several months Iris had been having run-ins with her foster mom who had learned that Iris was meeting friends during the day and was once again using alcohol and drugs, jeopardizing yet another baby in the womb.

Since she was also about four months pregnant, the authorities placed Iris back into the juvenile lockup in Jackson, along with Cierra, while they debated what to do. As much as it grieved me that Cierra was locked up with Iris, she was probably safer in the lockup than in a less supervised setting.

Cierra was fifteen months old by that time. She and Iris were in a twenty-four-hour supervised environment. The doors were locked and the inmates had limited access to the outside. It was then that, unknown to me, the state agency decided to end the experiment started by the social worker who took Cierra from our care.

All during those nine months I had stayed in contact with Iris and had given her my telephone number, telling her to call me if she ever needed my help.

One day I got a collect call from Iris. She was hysterical and it was hard for me to understand her at first. Then I calmed her down enough to ask her what was wrong.

"Oh, Miz Anglin," she wailed, "they're comin' to take my baby away and put her in a foster home in Detroit! You've gotta help me!"

I had suspected that this would happen—that the experiment would fail and the situation would be back at square one, when we gave up Cierra six months earlier. As far as the social worker was concerned, he reassured himself that at least he had tried to keep mother and daughter together. *But at what cost?!* That time that Cierra was in the care of Iris may have cost her something more precious than time. The social worker may have sacrificed the child for a principle—and a flawed one at that.

My first response was to calm Iris and try to reassure her that this was for the best.

"Now, honey," I told her in motherly fashion, "you and I have already talked about this. You knew that you probably weren't going to be able to keep Cierra. I know that it's a terrible thing to turn your child over to someone else. Believe me, I know. But it may be for the best, dear."

"Miz Anglin," she cried, "you don't understand. They're going to put her in another foster home. That ain't right. I want *you* to take Cierra. If I can't keep her, I want you to have her. You love her and she loves you. Please. They won't listen to me. They're comin' soon to take her away. You gotta help me. Please, Miz Anglin!"

"But Iris," I replied frankly, "they want to place Cierra in an African-American home in Detroit. They believe that she'll do better in that environment than living in our home."

"No," she said emphatically. "I don't care about that. It's not the best thing for Cierra. Can't you see that? She belongs with you!"

Iris may have been immature and still quite adolescent, but suddenly she was seeing things quite clearly. "What do you want me to do?" I asked her.

"Please come right away. I' been battlin' them all morning. Nobody will listen to me. It's like I got no rights in my own baby's life. They'll listen to you. You're like a momma to me and you're the only one I can go to for help," Iris pleaded.

"Please, Miz Anglin," she continued, "they're comin' right away. You've gotta help."

"I'm on my way, Iris. I'll be there as soon as I can!" The decision was already made as I hung up the phone and called my neighbor to come over to watch my children while I drove to Jackson. I also asked her to phone Harold at school and tell him that I was responding to a crisis with Cierra in Jackson.

By the time I got there Iris was totally out of control. She was screaming, fighting with the staff. She had even thrown Cierra across the room—not out of malice, but out of utter frustration and sheer helplessness. Amazingly, the baby was not seriously injured.

The staff of the Jackson facility was sympathetic to me and knew me from my visits to see Iris and Cierra. The staff informed me that the call had come from Detroit. Cierra was to be transferred to an African-American home in that city. I soon got on the phone to the agency to plead with them to let me take Cierra home.

The supervisor on the other end took a belligerent attitude. "You stay out of this! The state is taking the baby from the mother. You have no say in this matter," she snapped.

"What do you mean? We *do* have plenty to say in this matter. We're *involved* and have been for a year and a half! We have a relationship not only with the baby but with her mother."

The woman breathed deeply and said nothing. Then she said more calmly, "We're taking the baby."

I picked up Cierra. She was in really bad shape. While she was not seriously injured by Iris in the immediate crisis, she was dehydrated and in total emotional shutdown. She was almost catatonic—her formerly bright and beautiful eyes now stared blankly into space, right past me.

I went to the person in charge of the Jackson facility and told them that neither Iris nor I was going to turn over the baby to the Detroit agency.

"But you'll have to," she said. "We have a court order. We have to comply."

A van had been called with two burly security guards (who looked more like thugs). They came into Iris's room to try escort her to the van. Iris fought with them and screamed hysterically. Finding an inner strength that I didn't know was there, I raised my voice and commanded, "Stop it! Take your hands off my girl!"

The two guards stopped, let go of Iris, and stared at me.

"You heard me! Stop it. She's a human being, not some animal. Stop it right now!" I ordered. Then I went over to Iris and took her in my arms and held her tightly. She stopped fighting and collapsed in my arms. I whispered soothingly into her ear as I stroked her hair and held her close. "It's all right, Iris. I'm here. It's going to be okay. But you've got to calm down. Otherwise they're going to take you to a place you won't want to be. Now calm down and I'll walk you through this."

"Now listen," I told the others, "we're going to work this out calmly. Just treat her with respect."

One of the guards from the Detroit agency said, "We have to use handcuffs or a straitjacket if she doesn't calm down. It's the only way to control her."

"You won't need those things if you'll treat her with respect," I said. "If you treat her with respect she'll go with you. But neither of us is going anywhere until we both understand what's going on here."

I learned then that two social workers from the Detroit agency were there. The first one said, "Listen, we have our instructions. We're supposed to pick up her baby and deliver it to a foster home in Detroit."

"Did the mother give her consent to that action?" I asked.

"She doesn't have to. She no longer has the right to make that choice. We're going to take the baby with us," she said crisply.

"No, you're not. This baby isn't going anywhere right now," I told her.

The other social worker chimed in. "Now listen— you can deal with your questions later. This baby is going to Detroit *now!*"

I knew I had no "rights" in the matter except those of concern for the baby and to give voice to Iris's objections. That was enough for me. I realized that legally they could do exactly what they were trying to do. But that didn't stop me.

"Who's in charge of this case?" I asked sharply. One social worker told me the name of the person in charge and once again I took a deep breath and spoke to the two social workers.

"Don't do anything until I talk to him," I ordered. Then I went to the phone and called his Detroit office. Fortunately the person in charge was in and took my call.

"Listen," I began, wasting no time with preliminary small talk. "I understand that you've made the decision to take the baby and place it in another foster home, but that isn't what the mother wants. She wants the baby to come back with us.

"You know that in five minutes I can call any psychiatrist in the country and he or she will agree that this would be in the best interest of the baby."

"The decision has already been made," he said, avoiding the issue. Then he added, "Mrs. Anglin, forget about this. You're out of the picture. You've been out of the picture for a long time."

"Well, I am definitely not out of the picture," I replied. "I'm not going away. You can't dismiss me that easily. I'm not going anyplace."

He sighed audibly over the phone and took a breath. Then he launched into what sounded like a well-rehearsed script about the difficulties in making decisions that have an impact on people's lives, how the system strives to be fair, and he talked for several minutes about policy and procedures. He concluded with a firm statement that was meant to quiet me. "Mrs. Anglin, you have no legal rights in this matter. You have no right to intervene for either the mother or the baby. Now stay out of this. We're not going to bend on this matter!"

I paused to let him finish, then said quietly but firmly, "Okay, we can do this the easy way or the hard way."

"What do you mean?" he asked.

"The easy way is that you let Cierra come back into foster care with us, supervised by the family counseling and child welfare services. And I'm willing to drive round-trip to Detroit, one and a half hours each way, to bring this baby as often as you deem necessary for visitations," I said, anticipating his objections.

"And of course you'd want to be reimbursed for those trips to Detroit?" he said sarcastically.

"No. This isn't about money. I'll do it because it's the right thing to do for the baby and the mother."

"Well, we're not going to do that," he said. "I told you that the decision has already been made."

"All right," I said, "you don't want to do it the easy way. I guess we can do it the hard way."

"What do you mean?"

"When your people leave here with the baby, followed by the mother in the van in handcuffs and a strait-jacket, I'll be in the car right behind them," I told him.

"Actually," I added, "I'll be a few minutes behind them. That's because before I leave, I'm going to make a few telephone calls first."

"Are you threatening me?" he asked.

"Oh, no, absolutely not. This is no threat. It's a promise. I will follow that van to Detroit and meet you on the steps of the DCFS building. . .along with Channel 6 News and Channel 8 and Channel 12. And I'll also call the head of the Coalition to End Racism in America to meet me there," I said. "I'll make a few calls to mobilize my network and bring as many foster-care and adoptive parents as we can down to the steps of the DCFS building to demonstrate.

"What do you think will happen when all those demonstrators show up when the TV news crews are there? And wouldn't they love to get shots of the young mother in handcuffs crying for her baby, screaming how she wants her baby to go back to the foster home where the baby spent her first nine months rather than uprooting her again for your experiment. Can you imagine the coverage? It'll probably be the leadoff item on all three channels. If that's what you want, fine. We'll do it the hard way."

There was silence on the other end of the line. Then

he said curtly, "Just a minute." He put me on hold.

Soon he came back on the line and sighed again. "All right," he said, "you can have the baby."

My heart leaped inside me with joy. But I was wary. He had made me a promise once before just to keep me at bay, then reneged the next day. This time I'd be more careful.

I was not willing to take the chance of leaving the facility with Cierra without some kind of written acknowledgement out of fear that I might be arrested for kidnapping and that the social worker in Detroit might claim we never had such an agreement.

"Thank you very much, sir," I told the man politely. "By the way, will you kindly fax a copy of our agreement to me here at the Jackson facility? Just something simple—that you are in agreement with the mother's decision and desire to place the baby in the foster home where she was initially. The facility will need some kind of an authorization like that to release Cierra."

Within an hour a fax came that allowed me to take Cierra home with me. While we waited, I sat with Iris as she held her baby for the last time.

"Iris," I said, "I have prayed for you and your baby every day for the past year and a half. Would it be all right if I prayed for you and Cierra before I go?"

"Yes, I'd like that very much," Iris answered.

She bowed her head reverently and clasped her hands as a little child in Sunday school might do. I prayed for them in very specific terms, asking for God's peace and blessing upon both their lives. When I finished, Iris said, "I really like the way that you can talk to God."

"Well, Iris, you can talk to God, too. Did you know that?"

"No, ma'am. I don't think God would listen to me," she said sadly.

"Oh, but He would," I told her. "You can talk to God anytime you want. The Bible says that He delights in listening to His children."

"But I don't know how to talk to God."

"You know how to talk to me, don't you? Well, just talk to God the same way. That's how easy it is to talk to God," I told her.

"But you're easy to talk to," Iris replied.

"Well, God is easier to talk to because He knows all about you—He knows all of your problems—and He loves you."

"I'm afraid to talk to Him," Iris said in a frightened little voice.

"Why are you afraid?" I asked.

"I'm afraid that I'll get some real bad punishment."

"Well, Iris," I said reassuringly, "there *are* consequences to our behavior. I'm not going to tell you that there aren't. You already *know* that there are. But the wonderful news is, no matter what bad things you may have done, God will forgive you. If you're really sorry for all the bad things that you've done, you can ask Him to forgive you and He will.

"Think of that, Iris. You've seen your social worker's file on you. It's a couple inches thick. It has all the things on your record that you've done in your life. It says in there that you were arrested when you were nine years old—and you're not much older than that now. Just think of all the things you've done since then.

"Now all those things will stay in those 'earthly' files. But God can erase all the bad things from His files," I said.

Iris listened and looked into my eyes with her own eyes wide with the conviction in her soul. "I don't know. . ." she said.

I explained to her how she could be forgiven by simply being sorry for her sins and asking God for His forgiveness. I told her how to find peace and assurance through Jesus.

A seed was planted that I prayed would reach fruition as I left Iris and drove back home with Cierra.

The homecoming was a mixture of joy and pain. Cierra had no sense of recognition of our house or of any of us. She didn't cry as she had when we first brought her home from the hospital eighteen months earlier, but in some ways it might have been good if she had—at least it would be a sign of life.

When I bathed her I saw the signs of the physical abuse on her arms and legs and back. We also were told that Cierra had been kept in a dark closet up to eight hours a day because she was too hard to watch. And food was withheld from the baby as punishment. But again, I couldn't blame Iris. She was a child who was being expected to know how to be a mother.

During the many months that followed it became increasingly difficult to take Cierra to visit Iris. As the child grew, she became more headstrong in her resistance to the weekly visitations. Each visit was a terrible experience. Cierra cried, kicked, and fought every time we drove to Detroit to see her biological mom.

One day, frustrated, I told the social worker to bring Cierra from the car to visit Iris. The woman shook her head, "That's not my job."

"Today it is," I countered. "I'm supposed to bring her here. She's here. It's up to you to see that she visits her mother. It's my job to comfort her when the visit is over. It's your turn to be the 'bad guy.' "

The social worker was victim to Cierra's kicking, screaming, and hitting. She was even bitten by the little girl, but she learned a lesson in what visitation rights are *really* like! I had to do that once every week for three years.

I could tell that Cierra was afraid of these visits and it took every bit of emotional energy for me to calm her down afterwards. Even then she would often have a seizure on the way home or have night terrors following just about every visit.

When she was a little older and could talk, I asked Cierra why she didn't want to visit Iris. She replied simply, "She hurt me."

It was a long, tedious struggle to get Cierra to come out of her shell and trust again.

After three years and many struggles, we were notified at last that our petition to adopt Cierra was to be heard by a judge. After a last-minute confrontation (I'll tell about that later when I share Serina's story) the adoption was made final.

Cierra was born with all kinds of strikes against her, but she became a thriving, growing little girl who was making wonderful progress in overcoming those adversities. Then she was taken away, and during those terrible nine months, she was broken and hurt. She forgot how to smile and began to regress. When she came back to us it took years for her to heal. In some ways, she will never be completely healed.

Cierra still has many challenges but is making progress every day. Therapy helps her achieve what seems impossible. It takes lots of dedication and persistence but we find that it is worth the effort.

When beautiful little Cierra came back to us, God helped her. It really hasn't been easy but it has been rewarding to see her making such strides again. Today she is bright, cheerful, outgoing, and happy. She enjoys making up skits as part of her homeschooling and especially likes presenting her original "plays" to family and friends.

In her life journal is a photograph of Iris. One day she may ask about her. For now, we tell her only the good things we remember about her and help to keep the biological connection intact—to help her remember who she is and her heritage. I also continue to pray every day for Iris and hope that God is working in her life as well.

CHAPTER SIX

Serina

When Iris became pregnant only three weeks after leaving the lockup, she fell into bad company once again and began to abuse alcohol and drugs during her second pregnancy.

The child that she was carrying was another girl — a half sister to Cierra whom we wanted to adopt — but the two children had different fathers. Iris was fifteen now, but still a child herself.

Iris was really sick before the birth of her baby. She developed a fever that ran up to 106 degrees and she was hospitalized. It was hard for the medical team to know just how much damage had been done to the fetus, but they were concerned.

Because of Iris's problems the baby was born prematurely — and addicted to alcohol and crack cocaine.

Named Serina, the tiny infant weighed only a few pounds and a serious infection affected some seventy percent of her brain.

I became quite close to Iris when I cared for her first baby Cierra. She seemed to have confidence in us and asked if we'd also take Serina into our foster care as soon as she was released from the hospital, with the idea of adopting her as well as Cierra when the parental rights were finally terminated.

Iris wanted me at the hospital when she gave birth, and when I saw the premature infant born I was shocked at how small she was. I prayed that God would spare that tiny life. The baby was immediately placed in neonatal intensive care where she was put on life support.

This time, Iris didn't bother to visit her baby. Serina was so tiny that Iris was afraid to touch her. She apparently also felt it would be emotionally easier for her to abandon the baby at the hospital and not try to get attached to her.

When Serina was born she was not much bigger than a Barbie doll. Her skin was so transparent that you could see her organs beneath. I had to be careful when I touched the premature baby in the incubator because I knew that any pressure from my hand would rub the fragile skin right from her body.

Her eyes were taped and flash photography was

forbidden because light could damage her eyes. There were IVs attached to her tiny head because her arms and legs were too small to find a vein.

Iris left the Detroit hospital when the baby was born, but I drove there every day while Serina was hospitalized in order to be with her. The duty nurses were really helpful. They encouraged me to maintain a constant light touch on the baby and let me sing "Jesus Loves Me," as well as other children's songs, to her. I even recorded some of these songs on a tape recorder and asked the nurses to play them for me when I was not there.

At my visits I spent long hours just touching, whispering love, and singing softly to Serina. I wrote in her journal after an early visit:

I sit here hour after hour just gazing at your tiny, fragile body trembling in the incubator. This glass box will be your home for many weeks to come, but I will be close by waiting for the moment I can hold you in my arms. For now you fit in the palm of my hand. The doctors tell me that the chances of your survival are slim, and if by chance you do survive, you will not likely ever function beyond infancy.

Sweet little angel, how could anyone give up on you? I love you and I believe in miracles! I will stay with you and help you on your journey. You are a precious gift that God has loaned to us. He alone knows your future, but deep down within my heart I believe that you will be with us for a long time.

Bless you, dear baby.

A social worker saw me on one of my daily visits to be with the baby. She stopped me and placed her hands on my shoulders and whispered to me bluntly, "There are just too many problems for her to survive. You don't want this baby."

I replied just as bluntly, "Who else do you think is going to want her? Of course I want her."

The social worker and several of the nurses tried to get me to change my mind. "That baby won't live long enough to ever leave the hospital," a nurse told me, adding, "and if she ever *does* leave she'll be profoundly retarded. She'll never, ever recognize her parents. She'll need around-the-clock care. It'll be an impossible situation."

"If that's what God wills for her," I said, "He will give us the strength and ability to cope."

Another nurse, when the others left, came over to me

and said kindly, "What you are doing is going to help. Your touch and voice will make a difference. Because of what you're doing, this baby might have a chance to survive." That was incredibly reassuring to me! It made the ninety-minute drive each way to and from the hospital seem more worthwhile.

I am sure that some of the nurses must have felt this premature baby should not have been allowed to live. No doubt some believed that all the pessimistic pronouncements of the medical personnel were likely to come true. I imagined that some might even think it would be a blessing if tiny Serina could die a merciful death—something that would also eliminate a potential financial nightmare for the taxpayers of Michigan. If some thought along these lines, they were probably also convinced that even if Serina survived she would be nothing but a "vegetable" and could never function as a viable human being.

I can almost understand the "logic" that someone might believe that ending the life of an "already brain-dead" cocaine-addicted baby would be doing the baby and society a favor. But whether someone would actually act on such thoughts is another matter.

An IV bag was hung and its needle inserted into a tiny vein in Serina's leg that fed a dosage of a powerful drug into the baby's bloodstream. This drug, given in the prescribed miniscule quantities, was used to combat a specialized infection. However, if too much of the drug were administered it might inadvertently kill the infant.

The IV bag was hung and the drug started feeding into the vein, but, as we later discovered, at a high rate instead of the smaller dosage. If it kept up at that rate it wouldn't take long to do damage to the baby's heart.

If that happened and Serina died, there probably wouldn't even be an autopsy. Any one of a dozen problems on the life-threatening list for Serina could kill her. If the drug caused heart failure, it would likely be diagnosed simply as "natural causes." No one would have even questioned it—in fact, many of the medical staff even expected it.

So the IV continued to drip into the line attached to the baby's leg. Given the body weight of only a few pounds for the premature baby, and the high rate that the drug was being administered through the IV, it wouldn't take long for the baby to die.

But God intervened!

The force of the liquid carrying the drug through the IV had "blown out" the tiny vein in the baby's leg. The drug kept flowing but into the leg just below the skin. For forty-five minutes the IV kept running and filling the area under the skin and muscle tissue in her tiny leg.

Finally, all the liquid had collected there and was too

much for that small space. A terrible "explosion" of muscle tissue, skin, and blood—along with the pooled IV solution and drug—burst through the tiny leg from the inside. Ironically, however, this dreadful injury saved Serina's life because it kept the drug from reaching her heart and killing her.

When the incident was discovered the doctors were called to repair the damage. They attached to the bone what little leg muscle wasn't destroyed when her leg burst open. There was no skin to graft over the gaping wound so it remained open for a long, long time.

It took three terribly long months for the leg wound to heal, requiring a number of doctors, surgeons, therapies, and interventions.

By the time the baby was strong enough to leave the hospital there were still many medical issues to be concerned about. I felt that since Serina had left the womb early that maybe it would help if I carried her in a tummy pack close to my body to mimic being in the womb. I felt that this might help her feel secure and loved until the right "gestational" time—when it seemed right for her "to be born."

She had many seizures and other medical crises to deal with, and I was soon worn out caring for her. Here is an entry from my journal shortly after she came to live with us:

This month I've had hardly a minute to sit down. Serina cries twenty-two out of twenty-four hours! She is a very difficult baby to care for. She has had four outbreaks of lesions and several brain inflammations and I know that she must suffer terribly from the crippling headaches.

The wound on her little leg continues to be a concern. It requires changing the bandages four times daily and soaking the leg. This dear little baby is so fragile.

The visiting nurse is also concerned about the baby's condition.

Serina's older sister Cierra seems to be doing much better since she has not seen her mother for a while. When we talk about her, Cierra runs and gets a book for me to read to her, trying to distract us from having anything to do with Iris.

Coping with Serina's many problems was also difficult because this was taking place when we were having all the problems with our efforts to try to adopt Cierra—and both children required attentive, loving caregivers. Sometimes I felt like a split personality trying to give necessary care and attention to each of these wonderful but needy little girls.

I learned to pray on the run. Sometimes there was a lull between four and five in the morning and I had the luxury of a more defined quiet time with the Lord. Other times were more frenzied. The Bible says that we often cry out to God with only groans—that we can't even frame the words for our prayers. I know that kind of praying really well—having done it so much—but I also know that He understands our wordless cries for help.

When you are carrying a baby in a tummy pack all day until you go to bed at night, you have a constant reminder before you that this baby needs a connection with God. (Actually, Harold was my partner in this process. I'd carry the baby all day, then he would take over when he came home in the afternoon from teaching school and in the evenings.) This intense bonding and attachment went on for two years.

God does the work in the life of the child. We are only the facilitators. The key to seeing it happen is to *expect God to work.*

I sang to Serina faithfully and stroked or massaged her tiny body constantly, talking in calming tones. Eventually I could feel her tense little body relax when I prayed for her and sang to her. It felt to me as if we had a three-way connection: God, Serina, and me.

(The tummy-pack carry was highly successful and

now a number of different therapists are using my method.)

Social workers and physical therapists came to our home often to check on the well-being of the two sisters. When Serina was just a few months old this report was placed in her file:

From the neurologist:

In summary, Serina is a severely manifold handicapped child whose significant defects are in social, adaptative, affective, and cognitive development. Her upper extremities' movement, posture, and tone do not suggest significant impairment. However, with regards to the lower extremities there is evidence for significant motor syndrome dysplasia (cerebral palsy) as her being able to walk is very uncertain. I think that she will fall into the moderate to severe range of retardation, probably severe.

I am a little uncertain about the degree of impairment of socialization and its effect but see major problems that this, too, will be moderate to severely affective.

Prognosis with regards to epilepsy is more uncertain.

Another specialist described Serina as having several different seizures—sometimes up to twenty petit mal seizures a day! A Department of Medical and Rehabilitation Assessment stated:

> *Serina has cerebral palsy as well as other multiple medical problems, including crack cocaine prenatal addiction, history of herpes and encephalitis, seizure disorders, and developmental delays. It is important that the foster caregiver monitor feeding, especially for evidence of aspiration. In the future Serina may require swallow studies for evaluation.*

It seemed to me that her brain was "stuck" and she couldn't properly trigger her motor skills. The medical authorities told me that she had suffered severe brain damage at the brain stem and that this condition made all her problems "global" in nature.

Well, I had heard other experts say that most of us use only ten percent of our brains, so I reasoned that even if ninty percent of her brain were damaged, there was still hope! So I began to look for new ways to teach her basic skills. Serina had very weak sucking ability that made it hard for her to drink from a bottle. The rehab specialists suggested that we consider putting in permanent feeding tubes so that the baby could be fed through tubes in her stomach. I fought that idea simply because it was so permanent and closed the door to other possibilities.

I tried a form of oral stimulation. Rubbing the inside of the baby's mouth seemed to create new pathways for the brain to learn how to suck better. Using a toothbrush to gently stimulate her tongue also helped. As Serina got older and could take pablum or baby food, I discovered that by gently stimulating the outside of her throat I could get the muscles to swallow food—a major accomplishment. When the therapists visited and saw what had been achieved they recommended the idea to others with children who have impaired motor skills and trouble swallowing or sucking.

Later, when it came time to teach her other motor skills like sitting, crawling, and preparation for walking, I found that experimentation can cause the brain to "rewire" itself and make otherwise useless limbs or muscles work when there is no apparent specific organic cause for the failure.

I remember the time, after many months of constant care, that I felt we had turned the corner. Until this time there was no obvious "connection" between Serina and me. I was simply a familiar being that was always there. When Serina looked at me it was without any recognition or response. I was haunted by the words of that social worker that predicted that the baby would never recognize its own parents.

It was true. There was no sign of recognition. Her face was blank and her eyes stared past me. But one day we had momentary eye contact. It startled me. For a few fleeting seconds Serina had looked into my eyes and something sparked.

I was affected so profoundly that I called the neurologist to tell him about the event. He seemed skeptical, or at least disinterested in the significance of what occurred. He said, "Well, Patty, every mother wants that to happen. Sometimes they even imagine that it *does* happen."

"No, you don't understand," I told him. "The baby connected with me for the first time."

"It was more likely an automatic reflex," he stated.

"A mother knows the difference when contact is established and a reflex action. She saw me for the first time and understood who I am."

The neurologist advised me not to take the experience too seriously—that Serina's problems were so severe that it was highly unlikely that she could give such a focused response. I chose to believe otherwise.

Over the next few days it happened again, more frequently. From a fleeting look to a full five seconds. Then, slowly over the next weeks and months it became longer—first ten seconds, then twenty, thirty. Serina seemed to be saying to me, "I'm ready. It's time for me to be born now," and, "I know you—you're my mommy." After a while she was more and more responsive and I knew that behind those beautiful dark eyes was an awakening conscious mind at work, seeking to make up for a lot of lost time.

Still, the work was slow and painstaking. I recall writing in Serina's journal several months after she came home from the hospital with us:

> *You have stopped having seizures after*
> *almost six hours of one after another. Your tiny*
> *body is exhausted, finally relaxed, and I pray*
> *that you will have a peaceful sleep.*
>
> *I am afraid to put you down for fear the*
> *seizures will begin again and I won't be here to*
> *help you, so Daddy and I take turns holding*
> *you, but he is so exhausted after suffering a*
> *migraine headache for the past two days. So for*
> *now, you sleep, tucked in the front pouch*
> *strapped on my chest. This has become your*
> *home since coming home from the hospital*
> *three months ago.*
>
> *Sometimes I get so tired—I feel I can't go*
> *on. But then I look at your beautiful face and*

*know that I must. God brought you to us for a
reason. . .to love you, be strong for you, believe
in miracles, and speak out on your behalf. I just
hope we honor Him with the challenge that He
has set before us.*

*I am weary as I hold you tonight—
physically exhausted, emotionally drained—
but you, sweet baby, must fight for life every day.
My problems are so little compared to yours.*

*Lord, please renew my spirit, and give me
the strength that I need. Take the strength that
You bless me with and breathe life into this
helpless little baby.*

*Let our lives and this beautiful baby be a
testimony to Your steadfast love.*

It seemed that we had countless hospital and doctor visits when Serina was small. Amazingly, God used some
of these experiences to bring help and healing to others.

One time when Serina was hospitalized for a series
of uncontrollable seizures, I met Kate,[1] whose little boy
was hospitalized with a severe asthma attack.

As her little boy slept, Kate watched as Serina shook
violently with seizures that could not be controlled by
drugs. Finally she came over to the edge of Serina's crib
and said sympathetically, "Your little girl is so sick."

---

[1]Not her real name

"Yes, she is," I nodded.

For a while we just stood there together with common concern for our little ones. Then with tears in her eyes Kate said, "You seem to be so calm. How do you find the strength to deal with this? My little guy has such bad asthma that I'm always so worn-out. I'm so afraid that he's going to die. I'm scared to death all the time. Aren't you afraid that your little girl might die?"

I thought for a moment before answering, then said, "Well, I'm not afraid if she dies. I am concerned about what's happening and I'm afraid for what this poor defenseless baby has to go through sometimes. My heart aches because she has to pay for the mistakes that her biological mother made.

"I get worn-out, too," I continued. "But when I'm at the end of my rope I ask God to give me more strength. Every time that I ask Him for it He always gives me strength.

"I need special strength almost every day to deal with each one of my children because they are all distinct and have different special needs.

"But getting back to the question you asked me — 'Am I afraid that my baby will die?' — is probably the hardest thing any of us will think about," I said to Kate. She sat in the chair beside my rocker and leaned in to listen attentively.

"It would be terrible to think that I might have to let go of one of these dear, sweet children—like Serina here. I can't imagine ever letting go of her. But I trust God. I have faith that He knows what He is doing," I said confidently.

Kate shook her head and said, "I couldn't be that calm. I'd go crazy if my boy died. That's why I can't imagine how you can be so calm if your child died."

"Well, I'm not sure how I'd respond if that happened to me," I admitted. "But I really don't have anything to be afraid of."

"Aren't you afraid of death? Do you think that there's anything like an afterlife?" Kate asked. "I mean, I don't know if there's a heaven—I hope so—but I'm not sure. What do you think?"

"Well," I said to her, "I know that God exists because He's very real in my life. And I believe what He tells me in the Bible—that He's prepared a place for us after we die—a place where we can be with Him. If He should ever call Serina home to heaven, whether now or later in life, it should be a time for celebration because He is bringing her to the place that He has prepared for her. Earth is not her home, heaven is."

Kate sat back in her chair as if I had slapped her. "Good grief!" she exclaimed. "How can you say that? How can you *celebrate* a child's death?!"

"Because I know that I don't have to worry about their future or their care if they go to be with God," I said. "My baby will be gone, but will go to a far better place—where he or she will never be sick or hurt again. That's such a comfort to me. I dedicated Serina to God and made a conscious decision to place her in His hands. Once I did that I no longer had to worry about when her time would come.

"God allows me to face life one day at a time. He and I handle things day by day," I said.

"But you have such peace about this. How can I have that peace?" Kate asked. "I'm always living on the edge of the precipice. Every day I'm scared to death. I'm afraid that my little boy will have an asthma attack that might kill him before I can get him help, and that only adds to my feeling of helplessness."

"I'd be happy to pray with you, Kate," I told her. She knelt beside me in the hospital room as I prayed. "Lord, please give Kate Your peace and give her the ability to take her fears and frustrations and turn them over to Jesus." I also asked God to reveal Himself to Kate because I sensed that she seemed eager to know Him.

Then I shared with Kate what it means to be a Christian, how repentance and turning from sin prepares us for heaven, so that we can be reunited with our children someday. I pointed Kate to faith in Jesus Christ and asked her to pray the words of her own heart, confessing her fears and mistakes and asking God to come into her life. She tearfully poured out her heart to the Lord as we knelt between the two beds of our children.

As we rose from prayer Kate asked, "Now what do I do?"

I walked over to the bedside table and opened the top drawer. Inside was a Gideon Bible and I took it out and gave it to her. "Read this. It's God's Word. You can read it while you're here with your little boy. Read it at home. Look to the Lord for guidance. The Bible says, 'Ask and ye shall receive.' God will give you peace, comfort, and understanding as you need them on a daily basis."

Kate smiled. "It sounds too simple to be true," she said.

"It *is* simple," I said. "Jesus said that if we'll have faith as a child, we can know God and receive His blessing. Faith doesn't have to be complicated."

Kate smiled and thanked me and soon left. I never saw her again but I believe that she began her journey as a Christian that night.

I also believe that if Serina hadn't been as sick as she was—if she hadn't had so many things wrong with her—we'd have never gone to the hospital, and Kate would not have heard about how to have faith in Christ.

That's why I believe that Serina's little life has had purpose from the very beginning. Even if it had been limited to this single event with Kate it would have had significance and purpose. However, there have been *a number of such instances* when I have been able to share God's love, peace, and salvation with those that we encounter at hospitals and clinics. Several of the children's doctors have shared their own personal spiritual experiences that have come about as a result of Serina and our other children. Each of these wonderful little ones has had an impact on the lives of these men and women.

I have now come to realize that our medical schedules are often divine appointments, and understanding that gives me a perspective that helps me tremendously.

During that period of our lives it seemed that my days were a constant blur of one medical crisis after another. Between physical therapy and doctors' appointments for Serina I was always on the run. One entry in my journal says:

> *Just this month alone we have had sixteen appointments—and the month isn't over yet! This month Serina has had nine serious seizures and eight lesion outbreaks. She has also had five migraine headaches. We are*

hoping that the Paradoxin will help with the migraines. It breaks my heart to see this tiny infant suffer so. I spend hours and hours holding her as she cries. I have to believe that it makes a difference. There are times I get discouraged when I look at this frail body and wonder why an innocent baby has to suffer for the mistakes of her mother.

In addition to the seizures, infections, and terrible head-aches, we had a lot of problems with Serina's leg. It was the one damaged in the hospital by the IV that caused her leg to burst open. Because of the seriousness of the wound and its slow healing, that leg was shorter than the other one was. I started with an appointment with a skilled plastic surgeon. I wanted him to look at her leg, particularly the scar, and determine if the scar tissue needed more surgery and see if it was interfering with the normal growth of her leg.

The doctor felt that surgery at that time would only aggravate the situation and said he wanted to examine her again in three to six months. He referred us to an orthopedic specialist.

The bone specialist created a pair of soft foam braces that the baby could wear that protected her skin and prevented the "scissoring" activity as an unconscious response. Until then Serina's legs were so stiff that it was difficult for her to bend them, so she constantly rubbed her feet together at the ankles until the skin was raw.

Meanwhile, we were also trying to cope with the problems and difficulties relating to our wanting to adopt Cierra, Serina's older sister. We felt we were on an emotional roller coaster while we waited for the state to make their decision.

Then one day I received a long letter from Iris. It was written in the handwriting of the young girl—a letter from her own heart that reflected much of the pain, guilt, and anguish that tormented her.

Ironically, Iris was pregnant again—for the third time—and she was only sixteen years old. By now she had gotten past the formality of "Miz Anglin" and called me Patty. She wrote:

> *Patty,*
>
> *How are you and the family? I hope in good health. I'm trying to make it. I'm having problems with my pregnancy, but nothing serious.*
>
> *I don't know if you have heard but I do plan to give Serina up for adoption. I love her with all my heart and that's why I'm doing what's best for her.*

She needs someone who can give her what she needs. I can't do it so I'm going to do what's right. Patty, it hurts so much, but what can I do but let her have a chance? I can care less what people think about me giving her up. It's just what I think. Sometimes I feel guilty because of the decisions I've made so I try to think of her well-being.

I know that if Serina passed out on me or went into a seizure I'd flip out of my mind.

They said you would have first choice because you've had her over a year. That's one of the reasons why I'm going to go ahead and sign papers. I trust you with my babies and it takes a lot because my babies are my life and if I thought for a minute they would be harmed, ain't no way I would see them with you. But you proved yourself when you had Cierra. That's why I acted like that when they wanted to put Cierra somewhere else. The point is, we both love my babies just the same and they love you, so why shouldn't you have them both? Serina knows you. Sorry it seems like I'm pushing her on you. I'm just hoping you can adopt her. I will sleep better knowing you were going to.

> *Well, I wrote so much 'til my fingers hurt so*
> *I'll talk to you when I see you.*
> *Take care!*
> *Love always, Iris*
> *P. S. Give my love to my babies.*

Iris had agreed to waive her parental rights for Serina and the state had already started the termination of rights on Cierra that was necessary to be able to move forward with the adoption of both girls.

In court the attorney representing Iris for the child welfare agency came into the room. My heart jumped with feelings of apprehension. His very size and form was intimidating. He was a towering six and a half feet tall and huge. His deep, resonant voice was also imposing.

The state's attorney was there to represent the children. He made a motion to the judge that parental rights be terminated. The other attorney did not object but asked to speak.

His booming bass voice filled the courtroom even without using a microphone. He said, "Your Honor, we are not opposed to the mother giving up parental rights. However, I'm here today to plead for termination of the adoption process for this couple." He pointed in our direction.

"For what reason?" the judge asked.

"Well, Your Honor, I believe that these two African-American babies should be placed with a black family. How are they ever going to know that they are black when they grow up?"

The judge looked over at us. I shifted my weight in my chair. "Well," I ventured, "I suppose I could hold Serina in front of a mirror. She will know."

"Yes, of course," the lawyer shot back. "But how will she *feel* black?"

"I don't know," I answered honestly. "I can show her the mirror and her beautiful brown skin and gorgeous dark eyes. I can remind her how pretty she is and she will see that it's true. But I don't know how to make her *feel* black—but I don't know if you can either. I can help her understand love—our love for her, God's love, and love for mankind. I believe that *love* is more important than skin color."

The lawyer, in condescending tones, ignored my remarks and continued his argument for placement in an African-American home. The state's attorney did not seem interested one way or the other. Finally the arguments were at an impasse.

At that point, a thin, girlish voice spoke up. "Judge, can I say something?" Iris asked.

"Yes, you can," he replied. He asked Iris to come forward and be sworn in for her testimony. When she sat down in the witness chair to speak she did so with clarity. Her small voice was quite a contrast to the booming bass of her attorney but we heard every word.

"Judge, I don't know why that lawyer is saying that. I guess he's my lawyer, but he don't speak for me. I want Miz Anglin and her husband to have my babies. I seen her with my babies and they love her. And she loves them. Besides, ain't nobody who knows how to care for them like she does. They probably woulda died if she hadn't come and took care of them," Iris said plainly.

The judge then called on me. "Regarding this matter of her black heritage, how will you deal with that and her biological mother?" he asked.

"Well, Your Honor," I answered, "I grew up in Africa. I know its history and culture better than a lot of African-Americans. In a way, Africa is where my roots are as well. I plan to tell Cierra and Serina about their African heritage and help them find identity in the combination of African and American cultures.

"As to their mother, I have had a good relationship with Iris since we met. I've never betrayed her in any way. In fact, I've put her picture in the girls' life journals to remind them often who she is. We pray for her every day. We don't intend to write her off because I know that she loves her children. Probably the hardest thing she's ever had to do is give these children up. We won't take advantage of that and destroy that connection with the children."

The judge listened attentively then announced, "It seems to me that while continuity of a racial culture can be good, there are sometimes other considerations that are as good or better. In this case, since the mother herself wishes to keep the children in the Anglin home, I see no reason why we can't honor her wishes. The court approves the petition for adoption of Cierra and Serina by the Anglins."

We were ecstatic at the judge's ruling. Even Iris gave a small squeal of elation when the judge made his announcement.

I suppose the attorney felt he was doing the right thing by pushing for a placement of the babies with an African-American family. But to us it seemed to be a subtle form of racism. We fully believed that Cierra and Serina would be able to enjoy the heritage of their African ancestry even though they'd be growing up in our home.

Some racism is more blatant, however. Our daughter Julie was in seventh grade at a public school when she got these two new sisters. She was very proud of them and liked to take them for rides in their strollers.

At school there was a girl in her class who constantly made derogatory racist remarks to Julie as they sat in the back of the classroom. I can remember myself as a seventh-grader and would have been just as stung by the words as Julie was, but I probably would have kept quiet.

Julie, however, had turned to the girl and said politely, "Don't use that word to describe my sisters. That's like a swear word. I love my sisters and I'm proud of them. So please don't use that word."

The other girl was something of a bully, however, and day after day she continued to use the offending word, even adding smutty descriptions to her verbal abuse—not loud enough for the teacher to hear but plenty loud for Julie.

Finally Julie said to her, "I've told you several times not to talk like that. I've warned you. The next time I'm going to smack you!"

The other girl ignored Julie and kept up her racist tirade.

With that Julie stood up and called the teacher's name, then she said, "I'm going to do something that will get me in trouble, but I'm afraid I'll have to do it anyway."

The other girl uttered one more racial slur under her breath.

With that Julie turned and smacked the girl full in the face, sending her sprawling across the floor. Spontaneously the whole class stood, applauding and cheering.

They were aware of the racist taunts and knew that Julie had been putting up with it too long.

The teacher must have known, too. She seemed reluctant to enforce the rules but said, "Julie, I must send you to the principal's office."

Julie said, "It'll be worth the walk!"

In the principal's office Julie explained what had just happened, adding, "I know that you have to suspend me for three days for fighting, but I just felt that I had to do what I did."

Later the teacher told me what had happened. She said, "I had trouble trying to restrain myself. I really felt like praising Julie for what she did. I can't condone fights, but the other girl really had it coming."

I told the teacher, "We don't teach our children to use violence to settle disagreements. I don't know what to say about what Julie did to the other girl. But frankly, I'm proud of her for standing up the way she did."

The teacher's eyes twinkled and she said, "So am I!"

I am convinced that love has made a difference in Serina's life, in helping her overcome the many obstacles and handicaps that have threatened her.

As she grew up she continued to have numerous seizures. I was afraid that as she got older it would be more and more difficult to always be at her side when it happened, so she wore a helmet, even in the house, for protection.

When Serina began to walk I worried about her falling—even with her helmet she might get hurt. There were so many potential threats to her safety and well-being that ordinary concern had become anxiety and worry. I knew that these emotions weren't healthy for me. As I prayed about this matter I think that God gave me special wisdom on how to treat her.

I could spend my entire life anxious and worrying about her at play. But what could I do? Then I sensed a loving rebuke. It was as if God were saying to me, *You have trusted Me when you put Serina in the care of doctors and therapists. Don't you think I can watch over her while she plays?*

It was true. I believed from the very beginning that God and I had struck a bargain—that if I took these kids into our family He'd give us guardian angels to protect our little ones from harm. He had kept His part of the bargain for more than two years. Why wouldn't guardian angels be watching Serina and the others at *all* times?

I decided to be a careful and watchful mom but not someone who would smother her kids with worry. That trust in God's special protection has helped to give me peace of mind and a calm heart.

The doctors' reports on Serina after two and a half

years showed that there were still a number of problems. She still had poor endurance, and one doctor reported, "Her muscle tone is generally weak and she has low stamina. She is weak and tired most of the time."

Yet she amazed the medical experts with major improvements and her sheer survival. Serina confounded the doctors and nurses that had given up on her. With God's help she has developed into a bright, happy, witty, and wonderful child. She began walking, although it took her longer than most children to learn because she often had seizures that would "erase" the learning experience from her brain and she'd have to start all over again.

Her miraculous brain had somehow found a way around this dilemma and "rewired" what had been "unwired" by the seizures. Sometimes she regressed and had to begin again. She did so without losing her wonderful cheerfulness.

Our pediatrician told me, "If Serina had been brought up in the best rehabilitation hospital in the world she would not have turned out any better because of your methods." She referred to my tummy pouch in which I carried her "skin-to-skin" for the first two years of her life and to the constant loving reinforcement we all gave her on a daily basis.

With patience and repetition we have been able to

achieve a great deal of normalcy in her life. Today, Serina is a remarkable child. She still has frequent petit mal seizures, but her grand mal seizures have been fewer and more controlled. Serina is now able to do quite a bit and often astonishes her doctors, many who had all but written her off after assessing her chances at birth. She has even recently learned how to ride a bike and is becoming more and more active, like the typical little girl that she is becoming.

With daily therapy Serina continues to improve. She is another miracle baby who surprised a great many people. But Harold and I had faith in her recovery and development because we have a great God.

Patty and her mother in an African mission hospital

Patty's father preparing for surgery

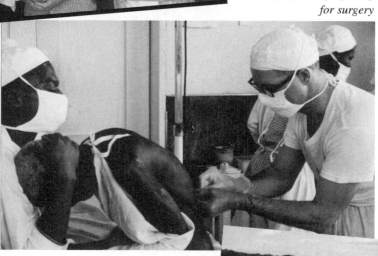

Harold—a true cowboy at heart!

Patty in the garden at Acres of Hope

Dinnertime at the Anglin home

*The lane
leading into
Acres of Hope*

*Homeschooling
session*

Serina

Ari

Serina—wearing a helmet to protect her
from falls during daily seizures

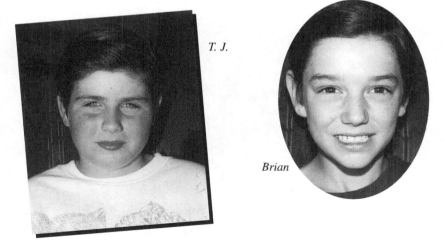

T. J.

Brian

Patty and Shawnee, who raised money to help bring Ari to the United States

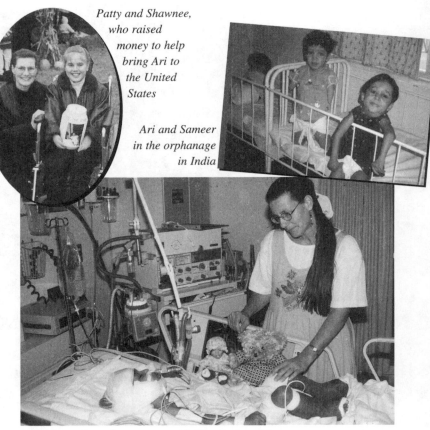

Ari and Sameer in the orphanage in India

Ari, after undergoing surgery, with Mom at her side

Ari—a citizen of the United States!

Tyler and Levi

*T. J. and Brian—
Brian's 7th birthday*

Tyler and Tirzah

*Serina, Cierra,
Tyler, and
Tirzah
playing
dress-up!*

Sisters—Cierra and Serina

149

Picture taken the day Cierra left our home to live with her birth mother in foster care

Brian's adoption day

Cierra three months later, the twinkle gone from her eyes

Cierra, just before her third birthday. She had been back home about a year.

Tyler loves playing dress up!

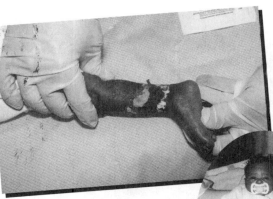

Serina's leg three weeks after injury

Serina, born prematurely and addicted to drugs, was not expected to live

Serina today with baby Zachary

Big sister Jennie with Zachary

Julie with Serina

A fun day at the pond!

A winter hay ride

Harold reading to his girls—
Cierra, Serina, and Ari

You never know where Tirzah
will take her nap!

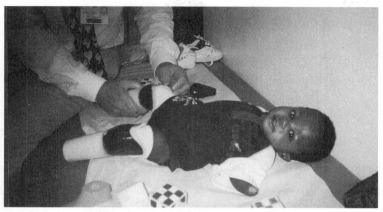

Zachary being fitted with his new legs

Zachary with his therapists

Cierra and Serina with big brother T. J.

The Anglin family with all fifteen children

Harold and Patty

CHAPTER SEVEN

Acres of Hope

As our adoptive family began to grow we thought about looking for a new home, one with more room and a bigger yard where the children could play. However, I was no longer working and on Harold's teacher's wages that seemed out of the question.

Harold and I had talked and dreamed about the possibility of moving to the West, maybe Montana, and finding an old small ranch and living off the land almost as the homesteaders did a century ago. Harold had a love for horses and other animals and felt it would be a good place to raise children.

However, a dream was all it was. I could never see a way for us to act on it.

Then two things happened to shake up our lives and confront the challenge of making our dreams come true.

First, Harold was approached by the board of education of the high school where he taught. As a cost-cutting effort the board decided to eliminate some of its teaching staff and offer some of the more tenured teachers an early retirement package as an incentive for them to quit.

Harold and I discussed the offer. It sounded good, but if Harold stayed a few more years he could add a little more to his retirement package and receive a higher monthly pension. Yet, Harold was not as happy as he was when he first began teaching.

Times changed, along with school policies. "Schools no longer have commonsense policies," Harold had complained to me one day. "It used to be if a teacher needed support the administration and school board would back him or her. Now every teacher is on his or her own.

"The school wants me to change my grading policy and give all As and Bs so kids can get into college easier," he told me. "But I couldn't do it. It wouldn't be fair to thirty years' worth of other kids that had to work for their grades."

Harold had also resisted the pressures for him to give passing grades to good athletes who hadn't earned them. "Teaching school isn't as much fun anymore," he said.

We were still weighing the pros and cons of whether to take the early retirement offer when I went to northern Wisconsin to visit my sister. Like me, she homeschools her children. Her children came together one day a week with other homeschool kids for special classes. They met in a small building built by the homeschool families in the rural community. These volunteers had built it with their own building materials and supplies.

Standing outside the building as we left, I noticed a beautiful farm across the street from the school building. "Wow!" I exclaimed. "If Harold and I could find a farm like that, I'd tell Harold to go ahead and take early retirement."

"Yes," my sister replied, "it *is* a nice farm. But it's not for sale. It's been in the family for generations. They'd never sell."

I couldn't blame them for not wanting to sell. There was lots of farmland, expansive woods, and a farmhouse (overlooking a magnificent vista) that we could almost see from the road. The drive onto the property was a lane nearly half a mile long, lined with huge century-old maples and red pines.

"Do you think that they'd mind if we drove down the lane to the farmhouse? I'd really like to see it," I asked my sister. Without waiting for her answer I turned the car onto the lane.

With their interlacing branches the trees were like a giant canopy covering the drive. There was an overwhelming sense of peace and tranquility as we slowly drove down the lane. As the drive turned slightly toward an old log home I saw an older man cutting wood.

I drove up near the place where he stood and rolled down the window. "I hope you don't mind," I told him, "we were just admiring your beautiful farm."

The farmer took off his cap and wiped his brow with a huge red handkerchief. Putting down his bucksaw, he walked over to our car.

"Ya, thank you. Vould you like a tour?" he asked in a friendly Swedish accent.

"Oh, we'd love it," I said quickly as we got out of the car. He walked us to the barn where he kept his tractor and some farm implements. We passed another building, a machine shed, with more farm equipment. Much of it looked rusty and unused for quite a while.

The farmer next took us behind the old log home and showed us the view to the east and said, "That's a million-dollar view, I tell ya. And over there," he said, pointing to the woods, "there's a nice hill where we used to have barn dances. You can see Lake Superior from up there."

"The woods look like they go on forever," I observed. "How many acres do you have here?"

"Yust two hundred acres," he answered. "Vould you like to come inside the house and have a cup of coffee?"

"How kind of you," I replied. "We'd love to see your house."

It was obvious that the old man lived alone. The house was neat but lacked a woman's touch. He picked up a big photo album and blew the dust off of it. "You can look at this vhile I get the coffee," he said. "There's lots of pictures of the farmhouse in there."

We enjoyed looking at the photos and were engrossed in them when the man returned from the kitchen with coffee and some cookies.

"I vas vondering," he said, "pardon my asking, but vhy do you have a black baby vith you?"

Serina was still a baby when I visited the farm that day, so I showed her off, and I gave him a brief summary of Serina and the rest of our growing family.

"I see," he said simply.

"In fact, because our family is growing, my husband and I have been thinking about moving to a ranch or farm like this. I don't suppose you'd consider selling your farm, would you?"

The farmer thought for a moment then said, "Yah. . . okay. I suppose."

Not certain that I heard him correctly I asked him again. "Did you say 'okay'? Does that mean you *would* sell it? I didn't think you'd be serious enough to actually sell it."

"Does that mean that you're not really interested?" he asked.

Dumbfounded I blurted out, "No! I mean, yes, I *am* interested. How much do you want for it?"

The old Swede smiled and asked, "How much do you have?"

Mentally I tried to fix a value on the farm. *Let's see, two hundred acres, a farmhouse, barn, and buildings, timber, grassland, cropland, and a beaver pond. Even at rock-bottom pricing such land could easily be worth a quarter of a million dollars.*

I sighed; there's no way we could come up with that kind of money. *End of conversation.*

But for some reason, a figure came into my head— it was a ridiculous figure, but it was probably within a range that we could afford. So I made an offer.

The old man rubbed his craggy face. I could hear the noise of his whiskers as he rubbed his face and considered my ridiculous offer. After a long pause he spoke. "I tell you vhat. Just for a little bit more, I'll throw in the tractors and hay vagons."

"Are you serious?" I exclaimed.

He frowned. "Yah. Do you have to check vith your husband?" he asked.

I laughed. "I don't think so. I think we've just bought a farm!"

I called Harold as soon as I got back to my sister's house. It was the last day of the board's proposal for the teachers to accept their offer of an early retirement. If the board's offer was to be accepted a teacher had to give notice before the end of that day.

When Harold answered the phone I said, "Honey, do you remember our arrangement to never spend more than a hundred dollars without consulting each other?"

Harold chuckled. "Don't tell me," he said, "you've bought another quilt."

"Well," I laughed, "I suppose that maybe from an airplane it looks something like a quilt."

"What are you talking about?"

"Honey, I just bought a two-hundred-acre farm. It's beautiful and perfect for our family. I believe that the Lord led us to this place."

There was a long, dramatic pause on the other end of the line. Then Harold said, "Do you think I'll like it?"

"Oh, yes! Definitely," I answered. "You'll *love* it."

"All right, then," he said. "Let's do it. You tell him that we'll take it. I'll give my notice right away that I'll accept the early retirement."

Harold and I had great trust in each other and he apparently felt he could count on my judgment in this matter. He didn't even have to see the farm to accept it!

By the time that I got back home and told Harold all the details about the farm, he asked the logical questions. The first, and most daunting, one was "Where are we going to get the money to buy the farm?"

I said, "Honey, I believe that God led me to this place and dropped it into our laps. I can't imagine why the farmer would sell it so cheaply unless God was behind it. So I believe that He will provide a way to get it."

Over the next few days I prayed long and hard for God's guidance. Harold had already accepted the offer of the early retirement package. That meant he would retire with a pension of about nineteen thousand dollars a year—about half of what he could have earned by waiting until age sixty-five. His pension was less because he chose to see that I was covered and could continue to get the pension if he died first.

A smaller pension meant that there was no extra cash we could use to buy the farm, or even to come up with a down payment.

On another visit to northern Wisconsin to see the property, I drove to a small bank in the tiny town nearest the farm. I asked to see the president of the bank.

A distinguished-looking man came over and introduced himself and asked how he could help.

"Well," I began, "I have sort of an odd request. You see, we're planning to buy a farm and bring our family up here to live."

I explained about our calling to adopt special-needs children and give them as full a life as we can.

"The trouble is," I told the bank president, "my husband is retired."

"Well, do you have the twenty percent down payment?" he asked.

"No. We don't have any money saved," I admitted. "In fact, we won't even be able to afford a mortgage payment unless we can sell our house in Michigan first. What can we do?"

"That really *is* an odd request. Do you have any collateral?" the banker asked.

I thought for a moment then said, "Well, we have an old 1968 Airstream trailer. I think it might be worth two or three thousand dollars. But that's all we have."

"Okay," the banker said, smiling. "That should be all right."

I was incredulous. "You mean you'll do the loan? I can't believe it."

"Yes," he replied. "This community needs more people like you."

With a commitment for a mortgage loan we could go ahead with the closing of the purchase of the farm. We put our house in Michigan on the market to sell, but there were no offers. Harold had lived in that house for twenty-seven years. While we loved it when we lived there, somehow it didn't have the same charm to prospective buyers. It took us two years to sell the old house.

However, in the meantime we were able to rent it out until it was sold, and the rental income covered the mortgage on that house so we didn't have to figure out a way to pay two mortgage payments.

The day finally came when we packed up all our belongings for the long trip to our new home. It took us fourteen hours to drive from Michigan to northern Wisconsin and after such a tiring drive with all the children it was so wonderful to turn into the tree-lined lane of our new farm.

I recall praying as we drove down the lane with our family for the first time. *Lord, this farm is going to be for children. This place is a vision I have as a safe haven for children, a place of hope. Acres and acres of hope. Yes, that's it! That'll be the name of our farm—Acres of Hope.*

It was so tranquil and the air was so fresh and clean, such a contrast to life in the city. The children began to thrive on this new way of life.

There was so much to do when we first got there. Over the next few months Harold worked harder than he ever did as a schoolteacher—at least physically. There were never-ending chores, repairs to be made, and lots of painting and remodeling to do. Eventually, it all began to take shape and our home seemed like paradise.

In the seven years that we have lived on the farm

Harold has expanded the old log home with additions going out from nearly every side to make more room for our growing family. Trees were cut from the timber growing on our property and taken to the local sawmill to be sawn into lumber for the construction. Other logs were dried and saved so that they could later be made into flooring. We acquired some animals—horses, a goat, chickens, geese, cats, and a dog. The older kids began to learn responsibility as they took care of the feeding and watering of the animals.

Harold has helped them learn how to farm. He and the older boys bale hay in the summer to feed the livestock in winter. We plant vegetables and do a lot of canning and freezing of the garden harvest. In the spring, when the maple sap is running, we gather the sap and make maple syrup. The season is short, just a couple of weeks, but we all work hard carrying buckets of maple sap to the kettles for boiling. It takes forty gallons of maple sap to make one gallon of syrup. The result is something like liquid gold.

On the hills above the farm are fields for running and playing, or simply hiking. In the nearby woods, just after Thanksgiving, we take the children to cut down a Christmas tree and carry it back to the house.

In another meadow in the warm weather, we erect a huge teepee for the kids to play in and sometimes hold their homeschool classes. Recently we acquired a school bus that also serves as a classroom for our children.

In the autumn we build huge bonfires to burn the accumulated brush pile from the summer activities.

Harold is still a science teacher—but now he home-schools the children in what we think is the world's best biology and botany lab. There are all kinds of plants and animals to study. Some days he and the older boys will go to the western edge of the farmland where there is a large beaver pond. They sit and watch the animals at work and play and experience biology and botany lessons firsthand as well as from their textbooks.

Or the children might see how swallows build their nests so precariously on the side of the barn. Harold can point out the habits of these various creatures and their unique features. He really knows everything about science. My lessons build on his. I tell the children how exceptional the birds and animals are—and how God created them with such unique qualities and instincts.

Recently a couple that we know who live on a nearby farm came to see us about harvesting rye. As we talked, Sally (the wife) told me of a strange dream that she'd had about our farm. Here is her account of it:

"Thirteen years ago I taught preschool in the area. I was not very familiar with the area because I lived several miles from the school. It was during this time that I had a dream, a dream so clear that it has stayed with me all these years.

"I didn't know where the dream was taking place, but the setting was very vivid and wonderful. In the dream I drove up a long, tree-lined driveway. It was so long that I couldn't see the farmhouse that I was coming up to, but as I came to the end of the drive, there was a huge house and yard full of children—it seemed to me that there were many children, all friendly, happy, and smiling.

"It was a 'good-feeling' dream, and I wondered where it came from. At first I thought that maybe it was a projection of my own desire to have a house full of happy children, but I had never seen that driveway and house before.

"Nearly a year after my dream, my husband-to-be was taking me to a lake that is beyond the school where I taught preschool. I hadn't been down that road before and was surprised that not far from the school was the very driveway that I had seen in my dream! I asked if there was an old farmhouse at the end of that beautiful drive-way where a family with lots of children lived.

"I was told, 'Yes, there is an old farmhouse, but no, an old farmer lives there all alone.' I suggested to my husband-to-be that maybe we should try to buy the farm and was told that the old farmer was not interested in selling.

"Apparently the dream was not for me personally. When we got married my husband and I bought another farm to raise our family on.

"Yesterday, when we went to talk to the Anglins about harvesting rye, was the first time that I actually drove up that drive. Yet it was very familiar because of the dream I had thirteen years earlier that I still recalled vividly!

"Then when I saw the farmhouse and all the happy children, it was an amazing confirmation of that unusual dream. I was so caught up in the wonder of it all that I mentioned it to Patty. Then we both understood that God has provided that place for the haven that it has become—a little bit of heaven in the rustic countryside."

The miracle of how God provided our farm still amazes me. Another neighbor told me recently that before we bought the farm the farmer had turned down an offer twice the amount that we paid and sold it to us at an incredibly low price. Only God could have worked in his heart to let us have his precious farm for "growing" an altogether different kind of crop.

Our farm has become a tranquil retreat for me. It has a wonderful calming effect to glance out my kitchen window and see a herd of deer grazing in the meadow to the south. I can observe the changing seasons by looking out my windows, too. The grasslands and hay fields begin the process by turning from green to brown. The woods are next and the maples, especially, illustrate the change with brilliant yellows, reds, and oranges.

We have lived on our farm long enough that I can see certain consistencies in the cycle of seasons and time. That reassures me that no matter what is happening to me now, things will change. I have learned to endure temporary difficulties because I know that in the overall scheme of things, there is always renewal of hope.

Another wonderful by-product of our getting the farm is that we may never have acted on the school board's offer for Harold's early retirement. It has given us the opportunity to *both* be *full-time* caregivers to our children. Actually, Harold is in many respects "Mr. Mom." He is really great at parenting and has wonderful wisdom to apply to every situation. I am so grateful for his full-time help. Without it I am sure that we would never have been able to bring these children into our home. Every day I thank God for this wonderful, faithful partner.

CHAPTER EIGHT

Ari and Betrayal

After our move to the farm we received information in the mail from an overseas adoption agency that placed youngsters from India. We looked at a photo of (then) four-year-old Arathi[1] and read her story.

We were told that Arathi was very fragile and had many medical needs. The agency had notified us because we had made known our commitment to adopt children that no one else would adopt. I fell in love with Arathi as soon as I saw her picture.

Little Arathi was born with severe arthrogryposis, a terrible disease involving her entire muscular and skeletal systems.

Mother Teresa's Sisters of Mercy had found the little girl—whom we immediately nicknamed "Ari." Ari was abandoned as a baby on the streets of a slum.

She was born to a young girl in India who had no

---

[1] Ari's Indian name

170

way to support her. I have no doubt that the heart of that young mother bled with grief as she had to abandon her tiny treasure and return to her village alone.

Ari was so tiny that she had to be fed with an eyedropper. Mother Teresa's nuns nurtured Ari until she was strong enough to be placed in the orphanage for adoption.

She languished in the orphanage for nearly five years waiting to be adopted. It was fairly standard for normal, healthy children to be adopted, while those with special needs were harder to place. The photos that the adoption agency sent of these special-needs kids captivated us. Her medical needs and intervention were urgent. She needed surgery and various kinds of therapies.

As an adoptive family we had a lot going for us. We were already multiracial and multicultural, and by now had years of experience. But the financial challenge of an overseas adoption was something we were not prepared for.

When we took note of the adoption expenses to bring a child from India, we learned it would cost about thirteen thousand dollars—money we didn't have. It would be a miracle if we could raise the money that was needed for travel and other adoption costs for Ari.

We were told more about Ari's condition (arthrogryposis) and how it affected her entire muscular and skeletal systems. Its effects also included actual physical deformity and paralysis. She was, in effect, a quadriplegic.

The muscles in her head and face were fibrotic. That is, they had no elasticity. As a result, Ari couldn't open her mouth more than a fraction of an inch.

She had rarely been out of her crib in five years, but she was bonded closely to her crib-mate, Sameer, a three-year-old boy born with a limb deficiency—he had no arms or legs. (We would meet him later.)

The biggest obstacle toward adopting Ari was the thirteen thousand dollars it would take to travel to India to get her and to pay the legal and adoption expenses associated with her adoption.

Soon after getting the information and photo of Ari, we shared our need with a neighbor. The neighbor shared it with another and another. It wasn't long before many people were calling and asking how they could help. Plans were made for community-wide fund-raisers. First there was a "Festival of Hope," held at our farm, that brought in about $1,400. Next, a pancake breakfast at the Lutheran Church raised $600; a spaghetti supper raised $850. An African dinner and musical entertainment evening featuring an African band raised $2,500. Churches of various denominations came together and helped out.

One special little girl, Shawnee Isham, was only twelve years old when she heard of Ari's adoption. She wanted to help raise money for the adoption expenses so

Ari could come to America. Shawnee asked her mother to take her to each of the local bars. There she told people that if they had money to drink, they had money to help Ari. She collected $122! Shawnee, although suffering from arthrogyposis (the same condition Ari has), amazed us all with her determination. Individual donations like Shawnee's amounted to $2,200 and were added to the fund. The response to this tiny girl halfway around the world was phenomenal—Ari had touched the hearts of an entire community.

But this is not to say that it happened quickly or easily. In all it took us almost two years and we were still six thousand dollars short of our need.

I was fairly sure that we could borrow some of the money that could be repaid over several years. The trouble was, we had used every available dollar to buy our farm and fix it up. We had no savings or other reserves. My father loaned me a thousand dollars, but we were still five thousand dollars short.

Things looked pretty bleak. I had no other sources to try to get donations or loans. *Lord,* I prayed, *can You show me where we can find five thousand dollars?*

Then—less than twenty-four hours later—the adoption agency called and the worker said, "I'm calling to tell you about a new fund that the agency has established. We've created a pool of funds to be used for low-interest loans to families that adopt special-needs kids. I'm calling to inform you that you qualify for a loan."

"Really?" I replied, "That's wonderful. We're still short of all the money that we need. What is the maximum we can borrow?" I asked.

"The fund will loan you up to five thousand dollars over three years at no interest," the agency spokesperson replied.

I was stunned. *Five thousand dollars! The exact amount that we needed.* I was excited to see how God works. He knows what we need, when we need it, and where we can get our needs fulfilled—even when we don't. He supplied the critical five thousand dollars at the exact time of our need.

Soon, we were making arrangements to fly to India.

There was one major obstacle, however, before we could leave—what should we do about the other children while we flew to India to pick up Ari? With their special needs it was not easy to find someone qualified to come and care for them.

Then, while I was talking on the phone to a friend back in Michigan, she volunteered to come up to

Wisconsin and stay with the children. I had met Della[1] when we both lived in Michigan and she and her husband were also foster parents. We met them through our foster-care network that had become something of a support group.

Della and her husband had previously lived near us and had offered on other occasions to baby-sit for us. They were foster parents who hoped to one day adopt children of their own.

One day Della told me about some problems they had with the Department of Children and Family Services (DCFS) authorities. One of their foster children, a girl of fourteen, was quite rebellious and promiscuous. She had asked Della for birth control pills and wanted a later curfew to be able to go out with her boyfriends. Della turned her down because her moral values would not let her dispense contraceptives to a fourteen-year-old nor let such a young girl be out late. According to Della, the girl retaliated and told the DCFS authorities that she was being physically abused and that Della and her husband also physically abused their two-year-old foster daughter.

Della and her husband were then investigated by the agency. The agency said that it felt that there was sufficient evidence that the couple had acted inappropriately and the DCFS authorities revoked their

---

[1]Not her real name

license to be foster parents.

I was sympathetic when I heard about their problem. It's not uncommon when foster-care families take in older children to encounter this kind of thing. An angry child, or one who is vindictive, may invent stories and make baseless accusations. Harold and I decided to take the couple at their word and support them through the investigation. Della was angry and bitter about this and declared to everyone that she and her husband were innocent of any wrongdoing and were being wrongfully accused.

When she had told me her side of the story, however, Della said that she and her husband had *voluntarily* turned in their license. I learned only much later that this was not the truth. However, during their struggles with the investigation we became good friends.

Several years earlier, Della came to me to write a letter of recommendation so that she and her husband could adopt two Hispanic children, a brother and sister that Harold and I had been foster parents of. I told her that the agency had already located a Hispanic couple that they felt was more qualified to adopt the two children. I was in support of the agency's decision. "It really is in the best interest of the kids," I told Della.

She got angry when I wouldn't write the recommendation and didn't speak to me for months.

She apparently thought that the "real" reason that I turned her down was because of the investigation. However, six months later she had gotten over it and called to tell me that she and her husband had given up the idea of adopting any children. "Our kids are almost grown and we should be thinking about retiring, not raising more kids," Della said. "Besides, I don't know if I can do what you and Harold are doing—with all those special-needs kids, I mean."

"Well, whatever you decide, Della," I said, "we'll still be your friends. I've been praying for you and I'll continue to support you."

She and I continued our friendship for some time after that. We'd visit and talk on a fairly regular basis, but after we moved to Wisconsin, there wasn't a lot of regular contact. We'd phone each other perhaps three or four times a year and maybe get together once a year when Harold and I were in Michigan visiting.

When the time came to go to India to get Ari from the orphanage and Harold and I were looking for someone to watch the children in our absence, we were greatly relieved when Della agreed to come to Wisconsin and watch them. Her husband had to work, however, so he stayed in Michigan.

It was a hectic schedule getting ready for our India trip. Harold and I first drove to Michigan in order to pick up Della and bring her to our home in northern Wisconsin. We brought her back several days before we were scheduled to leave so that Della might learn the various schedules of the children and have a chance to get a sense of our household.

My daughter Julie was sixteen years old at the time and had elected to go to a high school in town rather than be homeschooled. Her schedule was too busy for her to be of real help in caring for the younger children. It was probably best because in typical teenage fashion, Julie was not crazy about the idea of our adopting another child, let alone one from halfway around the world.

As I was packing, Julie asked if she could go with her boyfriend to meet his folks in Madison—a seven-hour drive from our home.

"Absolutely not!" I told her.

"But Mo-om!" she wailed. "He just wants me to meet his folks. Don't you trust me?"

I bit my lip before answering. "Look, Julie, you're not old enough to take trips with a boy. It'll put you in the way of temptation and I just won't let you do it. End of discussion," I said.

"Oh, yeah! You think all I'm gonna do is have sex!" she responded. "You don't trust me."

"Honey," I said to her, "it isn't right and I'm not going to put you in a compromising position. It isn't a matter of trust—it's just common sense."

The matter was put aside as I continued to get ready for our trip.

Della seemed extra attentive to a lot of the detail associated with our trip. One day as I was packing, Della asked, "If something happened to you in India, have you made any provision in your wills directing what should happen to the children?"

"Well, no," I answered. "I guess we haven't."

"You never know what can happen overseas," Della said. "You should call your attorney and have your wills indicate what should happen to the kids in the event something happened to you and Harold, God forbid."

"Maybe you're right," I told her.

"And have your attorney make me guardian of the children."

I looked at her quizzically. "Why?"

"Just temporarily," she added quickly, "in case of an emergency. If I had to take one of the kids to the doctor or hospital, they'd need somebody's permission in order for the doctor or hospital to treat them," Della said.

That sounded reasonable, but for some reason, in the rush of getting ready and despite Della's constant pressuring to have it done, I never got around to appointing her guardian of the children. But I forgot to tell Della that I had neglected to make her guardian of the kids.

On November 26, 1995, just after Thanksgiving, we left for India. Our flight took us first to Amsterdam. On the plane over the Atlantic I reviewed my hurried first entries in Ari's journal:

> *Today we left the farm in northern Wisconsin to make our long journey halfway around the world to bring little you home to join the family. The wait of over twenty-one months is finally becoming a reality!*
>
> *We are so excited and anxious to see India and complete the process of us becoming a family! Tomorrow we will get on an airplane and travel twenty-three hours. I just finished the final packing for the trip. We heard another snowstorm is on the way for northern Wisconsin. There were eight inches of snow on the ground when we left home. I wonder how much will be there when we get home. All of this will be so different for you!*

I took my pen and added some thoughts to the original entry:

> *November 27, 1995, 5:15 P.M.*
> *Well, here we are on the plane to*

Amsterdam, then on to Delhi! The flight to Amsterdam will take eight hours, then a six-hour layover, and another nine hours on to India. So far the plane ride is comfortable. I am so very tired, though, from all the preparation for our trip before we left. I hope to get some sleep on this flight.

I love you, Sweetie. We're almost there!

Mommy

We flew fourteen thousand miles and through twelve time zones. When we arrived our internal clocks were really mixed up and didn't know if it was day or night.

We arrived in Delhi late at night but the airport was packed with people—it seemed like the middle of the day (which it was, back home in Wisconsin). I wasn't feeling well when we arrived. No doubt all the hectic last-minute rushing around and packing, along with the stress of all the paperwork and visas, contributed to it. It was really hard to sleep on the planes, too, and after nearly a full day and night in a plane, I began to feel kind of claustrophobic.

We took a taxi from the airport to our hotel. I was overwhelmed by the sight of all the people who were walking the streets, working and doing all kinds of routine activities—in the middle of the night! The smells, sights, and sounds were all so different. The taxi driver seemed to have a knack for seeing how close he could come to pedestrians, other cars, oxcarts, pedal-powered rickshaws, and bicyclists without actually running into them. Horns honked incessantly and my jaws dropped when I saw an elephant walking down the expressway! What incredible sights and experiences.

We checked into our hotel at four A.M., totally exhausted. Knowing that we were only hours away from meeting Ari made me excited, and I didn't want to waste any time waiting to visit the orphanage.

In Hyderabad, our next stop on the journey, the orphanage staff received us with great geniality and courtesy—and we were greeted by the little ones who were either crawling or walking and seemed to be everywhere. The staff welcomed us and gave us a tour of the orphanage. We were so impressed that they could do so much with so little.

Finally we got to where little Ari was waiting. We quietly entered her world, the only one that she had ever known. Rows of worn white metal cribs filled the room. There were two or more babies or little children in most of them. In a far corner of the room, we were led toward the crib with a little boy and small girl in it. Staring through the bars of the crib was our little angel. At first glance at Ari my heart skipped and I knew instantly and intuitively that she was the one for us. I exclaimed to the director of the orphanage who was with us, "This is our little girl!"

As we gently approached Ari's crib, she became frightened and began to cry softly. I couldn't imagine how strange we must have appeared to her—people dressed differently and talking in a language that she couldn't understand. My heart melted when I looked into her gorgeous dark brown eyes. She was a beautiful child!

Despite my excitement and enthusiasm, my spirits sagged when I drew closer to her crib.

Ari, who was five years old, weighed only sixteen pounds! (On the information sheet that the orphanage sent to us her weight was listed at thirty-one pounds.) The full significance of the difference struck me dramatically when I saw this little angel for the first time. She was so tiny and fragile and in much worse condition than she was described.

As I spoke softly and soothingly to the little girl, she had a blank expression on her tiny, pretty face.

The director of the orphanage acted as interpreter. She spoke to Ari in her Indian dialect, then translated for us what Ari had said in reply. Ari couldn't speak even one word of English. I could see that we were going to have some troubles trying to take her home by airplane—a long flight without being able to communicate would be difficult for us both.

It was to take nearly two weeks to complete the paperwork for the adoption and get all the necessary government permissions, visas, passports, and other documents cared for, so we had a lot of time to spend getting to know Ari. By the fourth day, she began to seem more comfortable with us and was aware that she was going to leave the orphanage.

We really fell in love with Ari's crib-mate Sameer, too. When he understood that we were taking Ari he cried to go with her. If we had been permitted to take him along with us, we would have done so in an instant.

Over those next several days I tried to teach Ari a few key English words and listened attentively to the aides in the orphanage, to learn what certain Indian words and phrases meant. Yet that was still a long way from communicating on a practical basis.

We gave her the name Arianna and took her to Madras to process her visa. One of the aides from the orphanage, Rajene (herself an orphan who had grown up in the same orphanage), traveled with us to Madras. It took several days for the official paperwork to be processed and during that time we tried to become closer to Ari.

While we were in Madras I became very ill and had great difficulty in completing the routine work of the adoption process with the orphanage and Indian government. Fortunately Ari had bonded to Harold first and was content to be with him during my illness.

In addition to being quite ill I also had a sense of foreboding about our children back in America. This bad feeling persisted until I had to call back home to check up on them.

It was not easy to telephone them. It was difficult to use the Indian phone system for international calls, for one thing. The other problem was the difference in time. Being half a world away meant that in the United States it was midnight, while in India it was noon the next day. It was difficult to find a time that was fairly reasonable. To call Wisconsin where it was afternoon meant that I had to stay up until two or three o'clock in the morning.

Finally I was connected and I heard Della answer the phone. "Della," I said when I finally got her, "is everything all right?"

"Of course," she answered. "Everything's fine."

"Can I talk to the children?" I asked.

"Uh, they're all outside playing now," she said.

"Outside? In December? But we have heard the weather there is below zero."

"Well, yeah. They won't be out too long. They went out to the barn to play. But it'll take too long to call them to the phone," she said.

I sensed some nervousness in her voice. Then it

sounded like T. J.'s voice in the background saying, "Let me talk to my mom."

"Who's that? Is that T. J.?" I asked Della.

"That's just the TV," she replied. "No one is here."

I had a terrible sinking feeling in the pit of my stomach—I was positive that I had heard my son's voice and if I had, why was she lying about the children not being there? Yet I dismissed it as a reaction to my illness and some guilt for being away from my children.

Della ended the conversation by assuring me that everything was "all right" at home and that we should not worry. Still, I trusted my "mother instincts" that something was wrong—and seriously wrong at that. I had an eerie premonition to find the next plane back to America and get on it.

The next day in India my feelings of dread were as strong as ever and my illness had gotten more serious. It was diagnosed as dysentery and I could hardly function. After three days of a high fever, vomiting, and serious diarrhea a doctor came to see me. He provided me with some temporary relief but I was still quite weak and sick. Harold did most of the business in attending to the adoption while I lay sick in the hotel room.

We had planned to take several days after the adoption was final to do some sightseeing in India since we would probably never get there again. However, because of my sickness and the fact that by now Harold was sharing my uneasiness about the children—he also felt that something was wrong at home—we decided to find out if we could get an earlier flight back to America.

We went to the airline office and asked about pushing up our departure date. The clerk told us that for an extra four hundred dollars per ticket we could leave four days earlier. But at that point money was less important to me than the need to get back home to my children.

I boarded the flight in New Delhi and prayed that God would help me make it. We flew back from India with little Ari who patiently managed the first leg of the long flight—her first—with a sick new mother who had trouble understanding her language. Actually, she took to flying like a little angel.

By now I had lost eighteen pounds and felt more and more weak. When we landed in Amsterdam the eight-hour flight had proven to be too much for me. I had to get emergency treatment at the medical center in Amsterdam before continuing the flight. With the help of hydration and medication I was able to board the flight to Chicago to complete the second leg of the return journey to America.

Somehow we made it back across the twelve time zones and landed in Chicago. It was a week before Christmas and the outside temperature was minus forty-five degrees with the wind chill. Arianna had her first experience with winter but mastered the trip like a travel veteran.

Still suffering jet lag, Harold gathered up our luggage and helped Ari and me into the car and drove eight more hours to our farm.

We had called from the airport to alert Della that we were coming home early. Yet we were surprised to see her standing beside the door with her luggage beside her, ready to leave.

I was still so sick that things were almost a blur, but I was lucid enough to be puzzled by the stack of luggage. When she arrived, Della had come with a small suitcase and a little tote bag. Now, she had those but also had four huge black garbage bags full of stuff. I must have been staring at them because Della said, "While you were gone I had the neighbor come in a couple of afternoons so I could do some Christmas shopping. These are all my Christmas gifts to take home and wrap."

"But you're not going now," I said. "We just got back. Harold has been driving eight hours after little sleep on the plane. Can't you wait?"

She was insistent. "No; I talked to my husband and he needs me to come right away. I have to go now."

Harold helped me with Ari and we introduced her to the other children. They were so glad to see us that they climbed all over Harold and showered us both with hugs and kisses. All the while Della kept nervously shuffling back and forth across the living room, periodically glancing at her watch.

"I suppose I'd better take her home," Harold said to me. "Will you be all right if I leave you here?"

"Yes, I'll be fine. We're home now. I'll be just fine."

Harold took the luggage and garbage bags that Della had filled and carried them to our van. Then the two of them left for the fourteen-hour trip back to Michigan.

T. J. and Brian took it upon themselves to look after Ari and me as well as care for the younger children while Harold was gone. I had expected him to stay overnight in a motel to rest before heading back, but he turned around and drove back as soon as he dropped Della off at her home.

While Harold was gone, the kids came in and sat on my bed and told me incredible stories of abuse. "Mom, we're sure glad you're back!" said Cierra. "She was really mean—and crazy! She wore your clothes and made us call her 'Mommy.' She said that you and Daddy might not come back from India and that she would adopt us and be our mommy!"

The children sat wide-eyed and still somewhat frightened by the experience. The boys were still angry as they recounted how Della had hit them and locked them out of the house in the cold. I was overcome with nausea and tears. Not wanting to lose my composure in front of them, I asked the girls to go into the living room and play while Mommy rested, but asked Brian and T. J., who were older, to stay and tell me what had happened.

"She made us go outside and locked the door. It was so cold and windy that we got cold real fast but she wouldn't let us come back inside," Brian said. "We took the little kids to the barn—it was a little warmer there."

"And the day you called we were here. I wanted to talk to you but she wouldn't let me. She lied and said we were all outside," added T. J.

"One day when she made us go outside," Brian confided, "T. J. and I sneaked around the house and looked in the window to see why she made us come outside. Mom, we saw her going through your office and taking stuff out of the files and reading it. Then she took stuff out of the files and put it in some garbage bags."

I couldn't believe what I was hearing. I had trusted Della completely. I entrusted my children to her care. Now to learn that she had mistreated them, betrayed my trust, and invaded my privacy, I suddenly felt violated by Della and her intrusion into our family and home.

When Harold came home I waited to tell him. However, as he was unwinding from the terrible thirty-hour midwinter trip he commented about the strange ride.

"All the way to her home she seemed bitter and complaining. She kept saying over and over again, 'It's not fair that you and Patty can adopt kids and we can't.' Then she started on that old business about the investigation and how we let them down. Della said, 'We went through so much devastation but you and Patty didn't suffer a thing. It's so unfair.' I couldn't figure her out, but she's a strange, strange woman," Harold said, shaking his head sadly.

When the children told him what had taken place in our absence he felt the same feelings of regret and violation that I had experienced.

In the next few days I recovered from my bout of dysentery and began to look through my files and office records. I discovered to my horror that the children's birth certificates were missing, along with their hospital ID wristbands, photos, and other mementos. Also missing were critical letters, diaries, letters from the adopted children's birth parents, forms relating to their adoptions, the children's Social Security cards, medical records— *even their baby teeth!*

When I was putting away our luggage and clothes I discovered that some prize quilts and other personal effects were also missing.

As Harold and I discussed what had happened we decided it was serious enough to file a police report.

When the investigating officers came to get information, they were sympathetic but not very hopeful.

"Without bruises or other evidence of abuse, like some kind of proof that she locked them out of the house, it'll come down to her word against the kids' version of what happened. It'd be hard to file a criminal charge," the policeman explained. "And she lives out of state—that makes it tougher. In order to arrest her for the stuff she took from the house, we'd have to have a reasonable cause to get a local cop to take an interest, then convince the Michigan police to find a judge who'd issue a search warrant to go look for the stuff. Even if we did all that, by the time we got it done, she'd have stashed that stuff somewhere else."

"We've run into this kind of thing before," the policeman continued. "She seems to be acting out of jealousy and anger. It sounds like she set you up in order to sabotage your life. I think she took all those things to try to convince some agency that you intended for her to have your children. She could say, 'See, I've got all the kids' personal effects, birth certificates, and records. I'm really their mother.' "

A chill swept over me as I recalled Della's insistence to appoint her guardian of the children. If I had done so, I'm not sure how a judge would have sorted it all out!

The officer also told me that sick people often create

a copy of their own disaster and try to impose those same circumstances on the lives of others whom they blame to be responsible for their troubles. I could almost see a devious blueprint behind our troubles.

The police made a report of the incidents and put it into their files but Della was never charged.

As the days went by and I kept finding more things missing I felt more and more like a victim of emotional rape as well as robbery.

When the neighbors came by to meet our lovely new daughter Ari they told incredible stories of how Della had visited with them and began telling bizarre stories about Harold and me. The neighbors knew us well enough to know that the tales were lies and told her so. Yet several of them wondered whatever possessed us to have such an unstable woman care for our children.

When they left, I cried bitterly. I took on a great deal of guilt for what had happened, asking myself why I didn't see Della's "red flags."

I finally decided to telephone Della. I exercised tremendous restraint and tried to sound upbeat and matter-of-fact and not accusatory when I called her. After some preliminary small talk, I told her, "Della, the children told me that you hit them and made them go outside when it was really too cold to play outside. I don't understand why you would do that. . . ." My voice trailed off to allow her to respond.

"Well," she began in a voice heavy with sarcasm, "your kids are *all* messed up. They're all liars; you know that."

"No, Della," I answered. "They aren't messed up and they aren't liars. They do not lie, especially about something as serious as this. And even if they weren't telling me the truth, I'd know the difference. You see, I questioned them separately and got the same story. Kids that age aren't sophisticated enough to conspire to build elaborate lies."

Instead of responding to my statement, Della blurted out, "Why do you want to adopt another child when you already have so many? You've already got too many kids!" Then she hung up on me.

I called her back, but she hung up again.

Not long after that Della changed her phone number to one that was unlisted.

The effects of her betrayal left me with long-lasting emotional scars. For a long time afterward I kept finding more things missing and every one was a reminder of her bizarre actions. I also fell into deep depression. Harold and I sought help from a professional counselor and I struggled with the fact that it was my *friend* who had betrayed me and stolen irreplaceable files, documents, and articles. Yet worse than that, she had stolen my trust and friendship.

It took months of calling and writing to try to replace all she had taken from the files with copies of the original birth certificates, Social Security cards, medical reports, adoption records, and a myriad of other paperwork.

Harold and I were forced to relive this betrayal over the next several *years*. The State of Michigan began an investigation of us based on a thirteen-page single-spaced letter written by Della charging us with all sorts of malicious and falsified accusations. We were never given a copy of that letter or told what it actually said, but I am convinced that Della even wrote it sitting at my computer!

The accusations were made as an attempt to prevent our adoption of Ari from becoming final. It never worked, but for several years we had to live the nightmare that had accompanied what should have been a joyful event in our lives—that of adopting Ari. I regretted that the two matters had to be linked in time because the one forever clouded the happiness of the other.

It was almost as if Della had scripted and re-created how their lives had been interrupted and all but ruined as a result of the state's investigation of her and her husband years earlier. The investigation seemed to linger forever. It held up our adoption of Ari and once again we felt victimized by a sick woman, full of hate. Eventually the

State of Michigan ended the investigation, but the emotional fallout and financial toll were heavy. Although we were never convicted of any wrong, we had to hire an attorney to defend ourselves and after years of hearings, counseling, reports, investigating, and digging we were nearly devastated financially. It cost us well over fifteen thousand dollars in attorney's fees and other costs before the nightmare ended.

There was one more terrible thing that came to light in the aftermath of Della's time at our home. One day as Julie and I were talking about it she suddenly burst into tears and cried, "Oh, Mom, there's something else that I haven't told you."

I sat down beside her and tried to comfort her as she talked. She regained her composure and began to tell me the story.

"You remember when you told me that I couldn't go on that trip to Madison to meet my boyfriend's parents? Well, after you left for India Della said to me, 'Your parents don't understand you at all. They don't trust you either. I can't believe that they are such poor parents. I want you to know that I understand you. I trust you. And I'm giving you permission to go on that trip.' Since Della said it was okay, I went, Mom."

"And. . . ?" I was almost afraid for her to continue.

She burst out crying again. "It was just what you

said might happen, Mom."

My heart sank and I began to cry with Julie. We held each other as I tried to console her. Yet in another moment, my feelings of compassion for Julie were overwhelmed with intense anger towards Della. It was Della who was the guilty party. She had to know what would happen and probably hoped it would. It was yet another way to "get even" with me.

It took a long time for me to deal with that anger and hatred. I felt justified in my hatred because Della was the one really responsible for Julie's loss of innocence, not the two kids. Della stole something that Julie could never regain. I seethed inside every time I thought about it.

It took me a long time to gain a perspective on the whole episode. For several years I let the anger, frustration, disappointment, and betrayal eat away at my emotional well-being. I cried out to God so many times during this struggle—*Why, Lord? Why are You allowing these terrible things to happen?*

Then one day in my desperate self-pity it was as if God said to me, "You are forgetting My words— *'Praise the Lord in all things.'* " Was I supposed to praise God for the terrible things in my life as well as His blessings? The answer was obviously *yes*. Yet that was not an easy thing to do.

Then the Lord gave me another reminder—this one

from the book of Genesis where Joseph described his troubles and how God controlled the outcome. Joseph's brothers had changed their minds at the last minute about killing him—they "merely" sold him into slavery. In Egypt, an official's wife accused Joseph of rape, and although he was innocent, he was thrown into jail. Later, when he was pardoned, and was eventually made the ruler of Egypt. Joseph recalled[1] all those terrible things that had happened to him. "You meant it for evil but God meant it for good!" he said.

It was hard for me to see any good in our experience, but I've learned that God sees things differently than we do. I tried very hard to trust Him—so that He could bring something good out of that awful experience.

The most obvious good was that Della's betrayal bore no fruit. If its intent was to take our children from us, it failed miserably. If it was to make us give up on the mission that God called us to, it failed. Throughout the entire experience, despite all the depression, tears, hardships, and difficulties, God honored His own plan and preserved His integrity and ours while He foiled the plans of those who "meant it for evil."

There was a most significant way in which God "meant it for good." I learned firsthand what it means to be betrayed. There have been a number of times when that experience has proven to be helpful in helping our

---

[1]See Genesis 50:20

children and others. I can identify with those who have been betrayed and abused by those they have trusted. I can understand the frustration, anger, depression, and even rage that they feel.

Another good thing that has come out of my experience is the realization that I need to trust God implicitly and rely more upon Him. This helps me be more sensitive and helpful to the children in my care.

In my own case, I came to the conclusion one day that a great deal of my problems never went away because I had never *forgiven* Della. As I reflected over this lesson that God was teaching me I wondered, *How can I ever forgive her?*

With the Lord's help I made a conscious effort to forgive Della. It wasn't because I was some kind of a saint—quite the contrary! But I saw that the anger and resentment were affecting me and by allowing that I remained her victim. So I decided to forgive her and to begin praying for her, not because I had forgotten all the terrible things that she had done, but because that is what God expected of me. I still pray for her, and I still grieve for her. Yet, although she meant it for evil, God meant it for good.

CHAPTER NINE

Recovery and Growth

When the troubles were lifted from our household we could concentrate more fully on getting on with our lives. The most important matter at hand just then was the adoption of Ari.

It took two years to complete the adoption and we had survived many ordeals. Much of that time was due to the frustrations and difficulties brought on by the investigation by the Michigan DCFS triggered by Della's letter. It took a long time for the fallout of that nightmare to end.

There were some bright spots, however. While we were waiting for Ari's adoption to become final we told the orphanage in India that we wanted to also adopt Sameer, the little limb-deficient boy who had been Ari's crib-mate in India.

We were put on the list and we wondered how in the

world we would be able to raise enough money to bring Sameer to America to live with us.

We had been in touch with the overseas adoption agency and kept communicating our desire to adopt the precious little boy. I still choked with emotion recalling how he cried so plaintively to have us take him home along with Ari.

After several months of planning, the adoption agency called and the caseworker said, "I've got some news. We learned that there are four other adoption agencies that have been circulating the photos of Sameer to adoptive families. They had gotten no success, so that's why we contacted you. But now one of the other agencies has a family that wants to adopt Sameer."

My heart sank at the news. I recalled our decision to specialize in children that nobody else wanted. Now here was a clear contradiction. Somebody wanted Sameer.

"Tell me about the family," I asked.

"It's an orthopedic surgeon and his wife," the adoption agency worker explained. "They live in the Southwest and have already adopted one medically challenged child—from Russia, I think."

I thought about it for a minute. *An orthopedic surgeon is just what Sameer needs to help with his limb deficiencies and the need for prostheses.*

The caseworker continued, "I'm calling to tell you

that you folks have first choice. You agreed to adopt Sameer first, so unless you change your mind. . ."

I told the worker, "God knows what He is doing. Little Sameer couldn't pick a better family. We'll back out and let them adopt him."

I knew in my heart that this was the right decision, but it was difficult. We were already mentally prepared to expect Sameer was coming to live with us.

We grieved that it was not to be, but we all had a sense of peace that God was demonstrating once again that His plan is best.

We then concentrated on Ari. When we brought her back from India she began to thrive. Although she remained medically fragile, she began to gain weight and blossom in personality.

We discovered that Arianna had a keen mind and wonderful sense of humor. It took her just two months after she left India to learn fluent English when before she knew none!

Since Ari couldn't move at all, I tried to think of a way to encourage her to move something of her body — even to roll over. I got the "brainy" idea of positive reinforcement. She had never had chocolate candy before coming to us and she had learned to love it.

One day I asked Ari, "Would you like some chocolate chips?"

Of course she did and said so.

"I'm going to put you here on the floor and then I'll put these chocolate chips on this napkin here beside you. I want you to roll over so you can reach them. Then just pop them into your mouth."

"But, Mom, I can't *move*. I can't roll over," she said.

"I think maybe you can roll over," I said to her. "If you can, it will help you stretch your abilities in other areas. Just try it. Roll over so you can reach the chocolate."

"I can't!" she moaned and began to cry softly.

The other children were watching and Brian said, "Mom, that's mean! You shouldn't tell Ari to roll over if she can't."

"Yeah, Mom," added T. J. "You put the candy out of her reach. That's teasing her."

"No," I told them, "I'm trying to show her that she can do things that she never thought she could if she'll just try."

The boys got down on the floor to encourage Ari. "Watch me, Ari. Roll over, like this," Brian coached. The other kids began to roll on the floor, too.

Still Ari did not try it and the other children went back to their own activities. A bit later I went into the kitchen and after a moment or two, Ari's crying stopped. I waited a couple of minutes then went back into the other room. Ari had somehow rolled over onto her stomach and was able to reach the chocolate chips with her mouth. I had no idea that five or six chocolate chips could create such a mess of chocolate—on the napkin, the floor, Ari's clothes, and all over her face.

I laughed and went over to hug her.

She grinned sheepishly and said, "I did it, Mom. I *can* roll over!"

That rolling-over exercise was expanded to encourage Ari to move like that. If she could roll over once to get some candy, why couldn't she roll over several times and get from the sofa to the chair? She practiced and practiced and began to do well.

Then one day I announced, "Today, for lunch, everybody has to go to the kitchen by rolling on the floor to the kitchen table."

The smaller children thought it was a lark and eagerly got down on the floor. The older boys, however, thought it was a goofy idea. They had to be coaxed to set an example for Ari, and they got down on the floor and rolled their way into the kitchen.

Even Harold and I set aside our dignity and joined the kids. Ari took confidence at the rest of the family willing to move the only way that *she* could and made the effort. It took a while but she made it. We all cheered and clapped when she was by the kitchen table.

"Now we won't be doing this for every meal, but I

think it's important for you all to know how hard it is for Ari. And Ari, it's important that you see that you can do much more than you think you can. If you put your mind to it, there's no limit to what you can do!"

I think it was good to encourage her and give her confidence because Ari had so many things wrong medically. We began an odyssey of exams, consultations, and treatments. The various medical specialists deemed her muscular and spinal conditions the most serious and the lead surgeon of the team seemed to take charge.

When he examined Ari (then six years old) and conducted all kinds of tests, he determined a course of action that seemed rather drastic.

"Your best hope for Ari," he told us, "is to get her to be comfortable in a wheelchair. I'm afraid that she'll never walk. That's about the best we can hope for.

"Ari will always live life as a quadriplegic, even though her spinal cord hasn't suffered the usual damage of other quadriplegics," he added.

Ari, who had been listening, frowned and turned away. The doctor tried to chat with her, but she was quiet and ignored him. Her attitude had bordered on rudeness and I almost felt like apologizing to the doctor.

We left the doctor's office and I wheeled Ari to the parking lot, lifted her into the car, and stowed her wheelchair in the trunk. Then I got inside to buckle up.

"Ari," I said to her as we were ready to leave, "you were almost rude to the doctor. Why did you act like that?"

Instead of answering my question Ari asked me one. "Mom, please take me to another doctor."

"What?"

"I want to go to another doctor," Ari said.

"But why?"

"Because that doctor has no faith. He said that I would never walk. *I want to walk!* Please take me to a doctor who will help me walk," Ari insisted.

A few days later we made an appointment with Dr. Stig Jacobson at St. Joseph's Hospital in Marshfield, a three-hour drive from our home. Instead of making a decision right away, Dr. Jacobson examined Ari and did some tests. Then he consulted with some other doctors on staff. Finally he talked to Ari and asked her what she thought.

"I want to walk," she said simply. "Can you make me able to walk?"

Dr. Jacobson smiled and looked at her directly and said, "Ari, I promise you that I'll do my very best."

My eyes filled with tears when I saw Dr. Jacobson accept Ari's challenge to find a miracle to help her walk. All the other doctors had given up hope for that kind of improvement of her condition. We had even brought her from India with the full understanding that Ari would probably never walk. We ran the risk that this might still be the case when Dr. Jacobson finished with her, but at least she had some hope.

On September 16, 1996, we brought Ari to St. Joseph's Hospital for the first of many operations and treatments. While she was in intensive care following her surgery I wrote a few lines in her journal:

Ari,

> *I kissed your forehead and whispered "Jesus loves you" as they wheeled you through the operating room doors. Fifteen hours later you arrived in the intensive care unit where Daddy and I were waiting for you.*
>
> *Oh, my sweet girl, how I wish that I could go through this painful experience for you. I will stay right here with you, and your guardian angel will be with you, too. You are such a brave little girl, and we love you so much. We thank God every day for bringing you into our lives. Rest now, Ari. God will cradle you in His hand.*

Ari spent a total of fifty-three days in the hospital and some thirty-seven hours in surgery. Over the next year nine different doctors and surgeons attended her.

Countless days, weeks, and months of physical therapy followed her many different operations.

As her medical bills began to pile up I went to the hospital to talk to the nun in charge of the billing department. I told her our situation, then asked, "Could we pay something each month on the bills until they're paid off? We have insurance but they only cover eighty percent of the amount."

"Well," the nun said, "I suppose that will be all right. How much can you afford to pay each month?"

"Fifty dollars at best," I replied honestly.

The nun chuckled. "At that rate you will be paying fifty dollars a month until Jesus comes."

"Well, that's all right with us if it's all right with you," I answered.

I can't believe how patient and understanding the hospital has been and how we have been able to bring all of our children for all kinds of treatments, and there's never been any question raised about how much we might still owe them.

During all of Ari's medical interventions we prayed constantly. Never once during all those times did Ari ever complain about the pain or the discomfort of any of her surgeries or therapies. She was amazing.

However, none of the operations changed the fact that she was confined to a wheelchair and still as helpless as a spine-injured quadriplegic. Yet she has a vibrant faith and indomitable spirit. When she became an American citizen she was so impressed with the ceremony and wanted to hold a tiny American flag that she was given. I put the small flag in her hand and folded her fingers around it so that she could hold it.

Ari beamed proudly as the ceremony continued and she was declared "a citizen of the United States of America." My own heart welled with gratitude and pride at that moment. I completely forgot about all of our pain, anguish, and my friend's betrayal. There were so many horrendous experiences that had happened during our process of adopting Ari, yet now God had erased the hurt and given us His joy.

Last spring Ari was named as a spokeschild for the Children's Miracle Network and participated in their television special. It was a special time for us all as her story was told.

Ari is now eight years old and is a marvelous child. She excels in her schoolwork and delights in participating in the skits and plays that our children often present to visitors and friends. The other kids will dress her in a costume and roll her wheelchair to a prominent place on their "stage" and give their presentation. Ari's intelligence, personality, and wonderful sense of humor shine at times like these.

However, the thing I always remember most about her is the picture of that little girl in the doctor's office who had had the courage to ask for a second opinion and faith that one day she'd be able to walk.

The climax of that dream occurred quite recently as I was preparing to write this book. Here is the journal entry that records that event:

June 3, 1999
Dear Ari,

It's Mommy's birthday today and you gave me the most precious gift! You took your first five steps alone—without even your leg braces on. Three years ago the doctor told us that you would never walk. We know that miracles DO happen! You've had so many operations over the last three years, and will be having another big surgery on your hips in August, but we both believe that it has been worth it. When I asked you today if you really wanted to go through more surgery, your face lit up and you said, "Mom, no pain—no gain!"

What a girl!

Today Ari *can* walk, although right now (except for those few steps) only with help. She stands by leaning on a chair or stool and can take small steps if I hold on to her. But she says this is just the beginning.

"Don't you think I'm getting better, Mom?" she asks. Harold and I are beaming parents as we watch her work hard to take the baby steps that demonstrate her faith. We are both so proud of her.

Ari looks forward to the day when she can walk without any help. With her determination and the prayers of our entire family, I know that she'll make it— and that it will be soon! She is young, but she's also a veteran when it comes to faith and trust. Ari is a great believer in miracles.

CHAPTER TEN

The Miracle of Two More

In 1997 Harold and I decided that there was room for one more child in our home. We had barely come to that decision when I got a phone call from a Department of Children and Family Services agency in a city in southern Wisconsin.

The DCFS social worker called to tell me that they had three African-American siblings—two boys and a girl—who needed very experienced foster parents and adoptive parents to help them overcome major physical and emotional problems. It is typical in such cases for social workers to call on parents with experience to help evaluate the children.

We agreed to drive down and meet with them and to help evaluate the children and consult with DCFS about their placement.

There was a boy, age five, and two toddlers—a girl,

two-and-a-half years old, and another boy, eighteen months old. The agency wanted us to drive down and meet with them and also meet the children.

Harold and I agreed to do that but we had one concern. We had earlier made it a policy not to adopt any child older than the youngest one already at home. Older children almost always have a great deal more problems and more difficult issues to work through. In such consideration the most important thing is not to jeopardize any of the other children by bringing an older child into the home. This would certainly be the case with Michael.[1]

Although he was only five years old, Michael had exhibited dangerous and bizarre behavior. Social workers had documented cases of violent acting out that would suggest he was likely to do that in another foster home. Even the most experienced parents would be challenged by that kind of record and potential for violence.

Michael had been in seven different foster homes in his short life. Yet, he had never been placed in a home with his younger sister and brother. In fact, he had never even met them, let alone bonded with them as their sibling.

The two younger children, Tirzah and Tyler, did live in the same foster home, but Tirzah had lived in two different homes before her baby brother was born and the two babies *had lived in six different foster*

---

[1]Not his real name

homes in eighteen months!

The DCFS worker had hoped to place all three children in one home but was realistic enough to know that it was an unlikely goal. It was more likely that the older boy would not be adopted with the other two. The two smaller children had bonded as brother and sister and their problems were likely to be less severe than those of the five-year-old.

Those were the things that Harold and I discussed on our seven-hour drive to the city in southern Wisconsin where the children were being kept.

We rented a hotel room in the center of the old downtown district. It was a large enough room that we could bring the children there for play and get to know them.

After meeting with the DCFS contact at some length and discussing our concerns about the older boy, we were also told that this family was a high-risk adoption because the parental rights had not yet been terminated.

Harold and I agreed to take the children and evaluate them for the agency. We offered to pick up Michael at his foster home, but the caseworker was reluctant. She said that she'd pick him up, along with the other two children, and bring all three to the office.

When she returned with the children we had expected some dysfunction, but were startled to see how much. I first noticed five-year-old Michael. He was brought in and stood before us in an angry, defiant pose, glaring, with arms folded, almost daring us to interact with him.

Tirzah, the two-and-a-half-year-old, seemed more like a little baby. She had none of the curiosity or responses of a child her age. In fact, she had *no* response to any of the stimuli that were presented. Both Tirzah and Tyler had no expression on their faces, no spirit or energy, and their eyes were devoid of any emotion or awareness.

Despite her age, Tirzah was unable to do anything for herself. She was still in diapers and had a difficult time eating—choking on nearly every bite.

Harold took Michael under his wing and tried to get behind his shell. Since the hotel had a swimming pool downstairs Harold suggested that he take Michael down to the pool while I evaluated the two babies.

On the way downstairs Michael showed no fear of dangerous situations and was quite demonstrative. There were quite a few examples of highly inappropriate behavior that indicated to Harold that there was much work ahead to help Michael.

The boy showed absolutely no apprehension or restraint. If left to himself he would have climbed over the sixth-floor balcony rail or jumped from the stairwell landing. Harold had to hold onto his hand every second.

When the elevator at last brought them to the pool

level Harold took Michael over by the water. "Wow!" Michael exclaimed. "I never seen a bathtub this big before." It was apparent that he had never been to a swimming pool before.

Harold explained that the pool had two ends—a shallow end for children and a deep end for experienced swimmers.

"I can swim!" Michael announced, slipped from Harold's grasp, and jumped into the deep end of the pool. Harold had almost anticipated this so he was right there to rescue him. Michael sank to the bottom immediately and didn't know enough to push off the bottom to come up again. He just thrashed his arms and legs in the water that was five feet over his head.

Harold pulled him out and had expected that Michael would have a sense of fear or respect for the water but he didn't. Harold watched him very closely and kept him in the shallow end to play. There was some evidence of some sexual acting out that Harold noticed and it concerned him. Such activity would pose a danger to other children in a household. In his mind, it would not be in the best interests of Tirzah and Tyler to be placed with their brother in a foster home or for all three to be adopted together.

After spending a day with the kids, our hearts went out to Michael. He was no doubt the neediest of the three special-needs children but was probably going to be the hardest to place.

When we returned to the DCFS office we took a chance telling the social worker our evaluation, that it was in the best interest of the two youngest children to not be placed in the same home as Michael.

Agencies prefer to keep siblings together, however. In a perfect world, that would be ideal. In fact, they often use a hard-to-place child as leverage in an adoption. If a couple wants to adopt one of the children because that child, or baby, has fewer problems, the social worker will often say, "You can adopt this baby but you need to take all three of the children so we can keep the family together."

We learned that Michael had already experienced a failed adoption placement. To add to that disastrous kind of history made no sense to me. If a family couldn't handle Michael by himself, what made social workers think that an inexperienced family could handle Michael plus two other kids?

It would be better and less risky for Michael to be placed by himself and the other two separated from him. But it would be too disruptive—possibly even dangerous —for the other children to have him around.

I can't imagine the kinds of terrible things that must have happened to this five-year-old that would make him a sociopath even before he was old enough for school!

But such a history is not uncommon. We were told by the same social worker about another child, ten years old, who had stabbed his teacher.

We told the social worker that we were unable to help Michael but that we'd spend another day evaluating Tirzah and Tyler for the agency.

Harold was with me the next day to help in the review. He had not really spent much time with the two babies the day before because he was so preoccupied with Michael.

The first thing that he noticed was that they seemed to have a serious attachment disorder. They had not bonded with a mother or father figure, nor had they any input to give them a sense of awareness and individuality.

Neither of the children had any idea what toys were. When we placed a ball or block in Tirzah's hands she let it roll out onto the floor, not knowing what to do with it.

Likewise Tyler had no clue about what he should do with a toy truck.

Neither child knew how to respond to the most basic stimuli—patty-cake, peekaboo, singing, calling their names—it was as if they could not hear or understand anything.

Tyler had apparently shut us out completely and stood in a corner staring at the wall. In a little while, he began pounding his head against the wall. Harold picked him up to comfort him.

We were told that there were seventy-five pages of medical records in Tyler's DCFS file, many of his medical problems undiagnosed. Yet we could see some obvious signs of autistic behavior.

Two-and-a-half-year-old Tirzah could not talk as well as other toddlers her age. Most have a fairly wide vocabulary by age two, but she only made grunts and short whines to indicate something she wanted. She needed lots of special care in order to form attachments and make some progress in catching up with other youngsters her age, assuming there was no brain damage or impairment.

When it was time to eat, both children were still taking food from a bottle. Tirzah tried eating some strained baby food and seemed uncertain how to eat from a spoon but seemed to catch on slowly how to do it.

Tyler was not able to eat solid foods. In fact, I noticed that he had a problem in even sucking milk from a bottle. He seemed to have difficulty in swallowing and drooled excessively. When I tried to give him a small spoon of baby cereal he didn't know how to chew or handle more solid foods at all. He had the same problem as he had with the bottle—inability to swallow or even keep the food in his mouth.

Tyler had a front tooth missing and when I asked the social worker about that later she explained, "Tyler had an 'accident' and lost his tooth." The way that she used inflection to say the word "accident" let us know that it was a euphemism for abuse. Tyler had been struck in the face so hard that it knocked his tooth out. The abuse also left such nerve damage that Tyler was unable to control his saliva, which made him drool excessively.

The DCFS files confirmed that there was abuse in two of the six foster homes where Tirzah and Tyler were cared for. There was evidence, but no proof, that sexual abuse also took place. I learned that there were severe beatings, neglect, and worse in those two foster homes.

Harold and I agreed that the two little babies needed help and that we could provide that help. Reluctantly, we turned down the social worker's suggestion that we take Michael, although he was probably—if anything—more needy.

The social worker told us that a psychologist had determined that not only had Tirzah and Tyler never bonded with a parent figure, they had not even bonded with each other as brother and sister. They warned us that the children might never bond. However, we knew that even children who cannot bond can form some sort of an attachment—know who Mom and Dad are, know who their brothers and sisters are, and know their family by adoption.

Even if that is the best that one could hope for it is

important for kids, even if they don't bond, to see how and where they fit in a family.

Harold and I went back to the DCFS office and filled out the many forms and completed the paperwork necessary to take Tirzah and Tyler. We waited at the hotel for a social worker to bring them. He had done a lot of work with other kids with attachment disorders and had experience—not only with that type of problem but with other related issues as well.

I had been working with Tirzah and Tyler earlier to try to teach them the concept of play. I had given them toys but they could not relate to them or the idea of play.

The caseworker sat down on the floor beside Tyler and handed him the toy truck. After he finally got Tyler to take it, he snatched it away and said, "Mine!" in order to elicit a reaction or emotion from the boy.

Instead of trying to get the toy back, Tyler stood up and walked over to the wall and hung his head against it and cried softly.

"It's obvious that this boy hasn't learned how to try to get something back or relate to grown-ups," the man said. "I suspect that his situation is even worse than the little girl's. It might be better to split them up. I'm not sure, but I think there are fewer issues with Tirzah to deal with. It might be best to separate them."

I disagreed with him. "Look," I said, "these children

may not have bonded but at least there is a certain familiarity that they can build on. They've suffered together. I think we can build on that."

The social worker said, "I think you ought to consider just adopting the girl. Tyler has so many more concerns—both medical and behavioral. We've already agreed not to place Michael with the other two. It may make just as much sense to split them all up."

I continued to disagree with him. I had felt God impressing upon my heart that we should take both Tirzah and Tyler and I told him so. "Look, they both need God's hand on their little lives more than anything. I don't know of anyone more qualified to take them both and help them—do you?"

I knew that the social worker had tried every avenue before calling us in the first place so the answer to my question was obvious. He finally agreed to the placement of both children. "What could it hurt?" he said.

Approval was given for us to take the two babies home with us. As we were ready to leave, the social worker handed me a stack of files.

"Here are their records," he said. "You should find them interesting—maybe even helpful." I took the thick folders and stuck them into one of the suitcases and we left.

As Harold drove home I read from the files. It was

here that we first found out about Tirzah's abuse. Both of her little hands had been crushed and seventeen different bones had been broken. All of her fingers had been broken, and because they had not been set or treated properly, she had deformities on both hands. (Later, she would develop arthritic hands at the age of four!) X-rays showed calcium deposits on the joints of her fingers in both hands.

But the medical files left out a lot of information. The agency had given us the impression that these were fairly healthy youngsters. There had been no intervention services for them until they came to live with us. We knew that both Tirzah and Tyler were born prematurely and addicted to drugs and alcohol, but we didn't realize to what extent. Tyler, of the two, was more medically challenged. He had a seizure disorder for which he needed medication. He had serious hearing loss (no doubt from being slapped in one of the two abusive foster homes). Tyler also had hydrocephalia (as evidenced by a larger than usual head because of water retention by the brain).

Tyler was placed on medication for the nerve damage that was causing excessive drooling. We soon learned of his other medical problems: mild autism, attachment disorder, reactive attention disorder, fetal alcohol syndrome, cerebral palsy, and hearing disorder. The doctors say that he may also have suffered a slight stroke since one side of his body doesn't work as well as the other. They also suggest that the cerebral palsy and hearing loss might be the result of his birth mother's venereal disease.

The kids' files also had evidence of neglect and abuse, so the DCFS workers took them into protective custody. In one case a foster mother would not allow a therapist to come to work with one of the children. "That's an invasion of my privacy!" she told them, and wouldn't let anyone in her house. Another foster mother didn't bother to take care of Tirzah and Tyler. She left them to languish in their cribs without any attention—often letting them go a full day without being fed or changed.

Our seven-hour drive back home was exhausting. Both of the children cried constantly and did repetitive head banging for the entire trip. When we finally arrived back home at our farm we took the children inside to meet their new brothers and sisters. Cierra and Ari were especially captured by the two babies and began to hone their best mothering instincts. The boys held them and let them know that they were at home now and had lots of new brothers and sisters to love and help take care of them.

That night, when I was giving Tirzah a bath just before putting her to bed for the first time, I was horrified at what I saw.

Her little back was covered with scars caused by previous abuse. As I washed her hair I found small areas where she was bald. Someone had pulled her hair out from the scalp in several places. The DCFS files had indicated that Tirzah had done this to herself but I dispute that. Yet, even if she had pulled out her own hair, I couldn't imagine the desperate condition that would drive a little girl to self-mutilation in order to *feel* something. It was terrible abuse either way.

I could see that terrible harm had been done to this tiny little girl. I began to cry for her and tears streamed down my face.

Later that night I penned these words in Tirzah and Tyler's journal as its first entry:

November 8, 1997

I'm watching you sleep as I write this in your journal tonight, and my heart is aching, for I know you have not had sweet dreams as children your age should. Instead I know as I watch you toss and turn, sometimes screaming out in terror, that your short lives have been filled with the horrors of abuse and neglect.

Will your eyes ever have a twinkle, and your spirit dance with joy, or have the scars

*of your experiences carved themselves too
deep in your soul?*

*Today an eighteen-month-old boy and a two-
and-a-half-year-old girl, with lifeless eyes and
broken spirits, have joined our family. Neither of
you respond to your given birth names, so
Daddy and I will give you new names to start
your new lives with. Tyler Curtis is a good name
for you, my little one, for I believe that you will
be strong of character and educated to follow in
the pathways of righteousness. And for you,
sweet girl, we shall name you Tirzah Marie. You
have cried many tears and have had so much
sadness in your life; you have earned your
position as the delight of our lives and one day
you will bring protection to other lives.*

*It is with great joy that we welcome you in
our family today. As we step out in faith, we are
confident that God's mighty hands will be there
to guide us on our journey together. You are
loved, little ones. Good night.*

The next day when I took Tirzah and Tyler to our
pediatrician, Dr. Grace Heitsch, for their first exam I
pointed out the scars on her back, the bald spots, and
another scar on her chest.

The doctor said, "Patty, in order for her to receive a scar like this someone would have had to grab her breast and dig into it with fingernails and twist in order to do that kind of harm."

All told, the harm done to the children must have been fifty to a hundred times more than what was even in their thick DCFS files.

Both children suffered from night terrors the first few nights at our home. Harold and I took turns looking in on them. Several times they'd cry out, "No! No, no!" and scream. I went in once to comfort Tirzah, touching her head softly and whispering, "It's all right. Shh-h, it's all right." Instead of being comforted, she seemed even more terrified. She arched her back, stiffened, and began to tremble. I told the psychologist about this the next morning and she said that the next time that happened I should not be soft and reassuring but move right in and envelop her in my arms and hold her tightly, then comfort her with my words.

"She needs a deep-pressure touch to wake her up and get her out of her bad dream," she explained, adding, "The lighter touch may also remind her of some abusive behavior and that might account for the arching of the back, going stiff, and trembling."

The next time that happened I tried her method and it seemed to work. But I couldn't help myself from getting angry and wondering, *What kind of a person could be so cruel to a defenseless child?*

I suppose that to a certain extent we live in an "antiseptic" world, in denial that such a grotesque thing could happen. But it happens all the time, especially in homes without God. Most parents don't run into these problems and issues—and if they did, they probably wouldn't have a clue as to how to deal with them.

Since abuse of a child doesn't occur in most of society (fortunately!), we tend to shut out its existence. Even thinking about such a thing as child abuse takes most of us out of our comfort zone. But Harold and I have been out of our comfort zone for a long time, having faced these issues many times.

There are certain kinds of acting out on the part of children that are generally thought to be a result of child abuse. Both Tirzah and Tyler exhibited these characteristics. Tyler, in particular, would take off his diaper and smear feces all over the crib and walls (when he could reach them). It was as if he was unconsciously trying to make his crib as unappealing as he could in order to keep people away.

Since we think that most of the abuse apparently happened in their cribs, both of the children were afraid to go to bed at night. It became a real struggle at bedtime.

Tyler was still so small that I could keep him in the

"tummy pack" and carry him for six months. That forced bonding for half a year was effective in making a new attachment. During this time I wouldn't let any other adults hold him. This was a bit of a problem at church when a friend would come up and say, "Oh, he's so cute. Can I hold him?" I had to tell them, "No, I'm sorry. But it's because he doesn't know who he belongs to and will get frightened and confused."

Tyler had been left alone in his crib hour after hour in the first six foster homes he lived in. He was abused and beaten in two of those homes, so there was a lot we had to deal with in his little life. However, with the loving support of their new brothers and sisters and with parents who gave them the care they needed, Tirzah and Tyler began to get better.

Another journal entry tells part of the story:

February 17, 1998

It's been three months since you came home to start your new lives. There have been many doctor appointments and evaluations done. You both have been enrolled in the Birth to Three program. The therapists and doctors have not given us a very good prognosis for either of you, claiming your developmental delays are severe.

Tyler, you have been diagnosed with autism,

seizures disorder, severe asthma, reactive attach-
ment disorder, pervasive developmental disorder,
fetal alcohol syndrome effects, and static
encephalopathy.

Tirzah, your diagnosis includes post-
traumatic stress disorder (chronic), severe
speech and cognitive delays, sleep intolerance,
and trauma arthritis from the multiple broken
bones in your hands.

So many issues to deal with, it is sometimes
discouraging, but I want you to know, my
children, Daddy and I are committed 100 percent
to both of you. You have a lifetime to heal, so take
all the time you need, and in the meantime, we
will hold you in our arms and protect you.

Well, it *has* taken a lot of time for them to heal. Yet, they
have really blossomed in these past two years. But it has
taken massive amounts of physical therapy and medical
interventions.

Our pediatrician recommended a medication to help
control Tyler's excessive drooling. Ever concerned about
adding yet another drug to Tyler's regimen of medications, I asked if the drug had any side effects.

The doctor replied, "Well, the only one I can think
of is dry mouth."

"Perfect!" I exclaimed. "Let's try it."

For Tirzah, who has developed arthritic hands, the doctors recommended warm wax therapy. We used to have to go to the hospital or clinic almost every day and let the therapist put Tirzah's hands in the warm paraffin to help open and flex her finger joints. We have since bought our own warm paraffin machine so that we could do that at home. It takes an hour for this therapy and it needs to be done every morning.

I have also found ways to stimulate Tyler's weak throat muscles (caused by the nerve damage) in order to help him swallow. I tried some of the tricks I had learned when helping Serina learn to swallow—stimulation of the gums and tongue, and gently rubbing the outside of the throat when there is food in the mouth.

Tirzah is also getting speech therapy to help her with her language and speech deficiencies. She is making good progress and makes fewer mistakes in mixing the meanings of words.

The various physical therapies have helped Tirzah and Tyler tremendously. But the emotional help has given them a life. There is a rule of thumb that for however long a child is in a dysfunctional setting, it takes three times that long to bring him or her out of it.

We see wonderful encouraging signs of this happening with Tirzah and Tyler. They seem more like normal children now, having learned how to play and be with other children. They are personable, happy, and animated kids who love to play and pretend. It's exciting and rewarding to see them start to come out of their shells and blossom into functional children.

Tyler's seizures are mostly controlled now by medicines, and both children have fewer nightmares. Yet, if that rule of thumb applies, it will be another four years before much of their past suffering and disorders are behind them.

Interestingly, we have found a couple of "home remedy" therapies to do wonders. The first is the trampoline that we have in our backyard. I've discovered that it's a wonderful way for the children to develop better motor skills and coordination. When we first brought Tirzah and Tyler home to the farm we thought the farm animals would fascinate them. Tyler was frightened by them and at first didn't want to go near the barn. He was also afraid of the trampoline until he figured out how he could make it work by jumping.

After that, the trampoline has been a wonderful tool not only in helping his coordination and motor skills, but it has given him self-confidence and a concept of fun and play. (This in turn led to his no longer being frightened by the farm animals—in fact, he loves to ride on Billy,[1] our goat, or go horseback riding with Harold.)

---

[1] Friends tease us at the lack of originality concerning our goat's name, but I tell them that we used up all our creativity in giving our children their names.

I think it was Serina who was convinced that Tirzah needed a "laughter therapy" in order to help her forget all the bad things. I thought it was pretty perceptive at the time. As a family we looked for ways to make Tirzah laugh. Ari would think up jokes and funny riddles, Cierra and Serina would draw funny pictures, and we all looked for funny things on television or in magazines.

Tirzah began to catch on and looked for funny things herself because she enjoyed laughing. Once, when we were making arrangements to take Tirzah to Dr. Heitsch for a checkup, she came up with her own idea of a practical joke.

"Mom," she suggested, "how about when we go to the doctor's office I pretend to be Tyler and Tyler can pretend to be me? We'll fool the doctor."

"Oh, that's a funny idea!" giggled Serina. My own response was that children's humor must be on a totally different plane than ours. I didn't think it was all that funny. But I was thinking of how sophisticated adults are. So I decided to enlist the help of the doctor—and I called her ahead of time to tell her of the idea to make sure she laughed appropriately.

Then I got caught up in the joke. I took photos of Tirzah and Tyler to the photo store that was having a sale on poster-size prints. I had them make one of each of the kids, cut out their faces, and pasted the pictures onto a tongue depressor. When Tirzah held up the picture of Tyler in front of her face and pretended to be her brother, she laughed hysterically. It was also a big joke to the other younger children.

When we got to the doctor's office Tirzah went inside ahead of me. "I'm not Tirzah," she said to the doctor, "I'm Tyler. I'm really Tyler."

The pediatrician was supposed to laugh on cue but she was so caught up in the naïve aspect of the joke that it wasn't forced. It really was *funny* and we both began to laugh along with the kids. In fact, we probably got too carried away, judging by the strange looks from the other mothers in the waiting room who heard the uproar and stared at us when we left.

Tirzah talked about the joke for weeks after that and I could see the real value of the "laughing therapy."

The parental rights termination for Tirzah and Tyler took over a year to be finalized. During this time the social workers made frequent visits to our home and brought more and more paperwork for us to complete. After all the delays, disruptions, and legal maneuvers, the adoption proceedings were at last completed. Tirzah and Tyler are now officially our adopted children.

My journal entry for them on Christmas Eve 1998 still makes me smile as I recall the children's program in church that night:

The Christmas program at church tonight was wonderful. I was so proud of you, Tirzah! You sang all the songs, and you stood there so nicely. (I loved it when you waved to me, then blew me a kiss!) How pretty you looked all dressed up in your Christmas dress, but the most wonderful thing was your smile. A year ago you didn't know how to smile. As I watched you up there on stage, I remembered the scared little girl with no spirit. What a change! You are like a flower unfolding!

And Tyler, why shouldn't *you be in the Christmas program? Just because the script didn't call for you to run up the aisle, take the microphone, and yell "Hi!" doesn't mean that the play wasn't actually improved by your involvement! I was delighted that you wanted to be a part of the night. You had that long-awaited twinkle in your eyes; the twinkle that I had dreamed of seeing since you came into our lives. When we got home from church and I was getting you ready for bed, you looked up at me and asked, "Jesus love me?" You are absolutely a wonder. How exciting to hear your first words and that they would be about Jesus! And yes, Tyler, Jesus* does *love you.*

All the pain and difficulties are gradually fading from our memories as we celebrate Tirzah's and Tyler's permanence in our family. In fact, I sometimes have to force myself to recall the bad things because so many good things surround us now.

CHAPTER ELEVEN

Little Levi

Guardian angels were on duty January 8, 1997, in Cincinnati, Ohio. In a slum apartment a twenty-seven-year-old woman was drunk but had enough of her faculties to know that she was about to give birth.

This would be her seventh child. Every one of the others had been placed in foster homes or adopted. This time she was confused and befuddled by alcohol. Somehow she gave birth to the baby—a boy, born prematurely and suffering from fetal alcohol syndrome (FAS).

The mother did not want to keep this baby either. She also apparently didn't want to go through the hassle of notifying the DCFS or other authorities. In any event, she wrapped the tiny baby in a towel and left the apartment, looking for a place to abandon the baby. Checking to make sure that no one was watching, she tossed him into a nearby Dumpster.

The weather that day was sub-freezing with the wind chill. The tiny little infant would have frozen to death in hardly any time at all but for the grace of God.

A policeman, after receiving a call from a concerned neighbor, came to the area to check out a complaint. For some reason he checked the Dumpster, where he discovered the baby. Immediately he gave the infant mouth-to-mouth resuscitation to breathe life into its seemingly lifeless form. When he saw shallow breathing he put the baby inside his shirt next to his own body for warmth and called in the report of the abandoned baby.

The policeman rushed the baby to a downtown hospital. When the emergency room medics took the baby's vital signs, the infant's weight was just four pounds and *his body temperature was nearly at the freezing point!*

The doctors put the baby on life support and in a special warming incubator. When the baby's blood was tested, it showed that he was *actually drunk!* (No one ever told me, but I wonder if the alcohol in his blood is what kept his body from freezing.)

Whatever the case, I really believe that God led that policeman to the Dumpster and saved his life—the first of many life-threatening events when the Lord performed more miracles.

A conference of medical personnel at the hospital

confirmed that the baby was born with FAS, so he had to be carefully monitored and treated. The infant was kept in the hospital neonatal intensive care section for several weeks before being turned over to foster care.

The baby was listed officially as a "John Doe" with unknown parents (we later named him Levi). However, in the emergency rush to give him vital care the hospital had neglected to give him a birth certificate.

The doctors were concentrating on finding out the problems threatening the life of Levi. Tests indicated that in addition to alcohol, the baby was addicted to *five other drugs!*—including cocaine. Yet as bad as these other drugs were, alcohol was by far the worst villain in the drama.

Levi's most serious problems were the result of his mother's drinking. It was likely that she drank to excess *almost every day of her pregnancy.*

That means that his birth mother gave Levi a terrible legacy of mental impairment, learning disorders, physical impairments, and a whole litany of other problems.

Levi was also born with an infectious sexually transmitted disease from his mother, but, thankfully, with prompt, effective treatment he was cured.

Of course, all this had taken place before I had ever heard of Levi. It wasn't until several months later that we came into the picture.

A sensitive, loving social worker from Cincinnati called me about Levi a few months after his birth. After sharing his story with me she said, "Patty, I know that you've had a great deal of experience with fetal alcohol syndrome (FAS) babies. I'm really afraid for this infant. There are so few people who can handle an FAS baby like this. I thought you might be able to help me find a foster home or adoptive couple for him."

"I'll do my best," I offered and got out my Rolodex and began making calls. I knew it would be difficult because couples who want to adopt are often shy about adopting special-needs children. In the case of FAS, it is difficult to predict the full extent of the problems or how far the child might progress.

The fetal alcohol child is usually mentally impaired, impulsive, hyperactive, easily distracted, does not learn from consequences, and is hard to impress about dangers. These children require much more attention to safety and more supervision. FAS babies don't grow up to think analytically, and learn only from constant repetition. They don't retain things in their memory from day to day. In many cases FAS children will, for the most part, always need to live at home and are usually unable to be independent unless it is in a group home.

These obstacles were too formidable for most young couples looking to adopt. I kept trying, though. I finally found a couple in our church whom I thought was willing to commit to him, but the timing for an adoption in their family was not right. So as I sought to find an adoptive couple I drew rejection after rejection.

Levi's foster parents poured themselves into giving the baby a loving home. This couple proved to be wonderful in giving Levi the strong emotional support that he needed. The most pressing concern with FAS babies is that they often have attachment disorders, meaning that it is sometimes impossible for them to bond with a parent or other adult.

In the case of Levi, however, he bonded wonderfully with this couple—an African-American minister and his wife. Yet, they did not adopt him.

After six months of searching I still had not found a couple willing to adopt Levi. I prayed, "Lord, I don't understand why it is so difficult finding a home and family for Levi. I know that it means a lifetime of commitment, and that scares a lot of people, but for the sake of this baby, he needs a loving home. Why haven't I been able to find Levi a home?"

At that moment I had an experience of great clarity. It was almost as if God had spoken aloud—*That's because Levi is your child.*

I talked with Harold about the possibility of our adopting Levi. We evaluated the situation and made a decision with our hearts. I called the social worker in Ohio and said simply, "You know, *I'll* take Levi."

She replied, "Oh, Patty, that's great! You were my first choice all along. No one knows more about FAS kids than you and your husband. I think that you told me once that all of your adopted children have FAS symptoms to some degree or another. I'll get right on it."

Since the baby had been abandoned the termination of parental rights had already been done, and that made the process less complicated. Still, the adoption took a year. In addition to all the problems and potential problems with this fetal alcohol baby, there were other medical difficulties. Levi was assessed with a "failure to thrive" evaluation, with seizures and tremors. There was also a question about existing or potential kidney failure.

Levi came to live with us in July 1998, as a frail nineteen-month-old who looked more like a six-month-old.

Here is my first entry in Levi's life journal:

July 26, 1998
Dear Levi,
    If ever there was a little boy who deserved to be chosen and loved, it is you, my son. My heart

*swells with delight that we have found each
other. I have spent a long time searching for just
the right family for you to grow up in—a family
that would not just love you and meet all your
medical needs, but one that would bring you up
in the ways of the Lord, teach you of His mighty
love, and believe as I do that you will be a
blessing to all those you come in contact with.
The Lord shut the door on family after family.
Why? I asked myself over and over. And then,
God spoke to me—that I had been looking and
searching in vain!*

*God showed me that you were to be OUR
son, our little angel.*

*There are so many wonderful experiences
that your life has to hold. Take each challenge
and look at it as an opportunity for growth.
Right now you have no idea of all that the world
has to offer. As you grow, you will spread your
wings. You may not always know which path to
follow, but if you learn to rely upon God for
guidance, He will help you.*

*Levi, you have a magical smile that has won
my heart. You are so small, so sweet, and trust-
ing. I pray that our bond will grow strong in the
years to come and that our journey together will*

be filled with many blessings.
I love you, Levi Tucker Anglin!
Forever and always, Mommy

The loving couple (the minister and his wife) had given Levi good emotional support while they were his foster parents. They showered him with love and Levi had bonded with them. But they were inexperienced with all of the medical issues with FAS babies and overwhelmed with meeting just the ordinary day-to-day needs. They did not understand the need for early intervention and therapy.

When I took Levi for a medical evaluation, one of the first things the doctors wanted to do was to surgically put in a permanent feeding tube because of his premature birth and "failure to thrive" diagnosis that had caused his small size and low weight as well as the difficulty in eating.

I didn't like the idea of such a permanent action at Levi's young age. I asked if I could try to help Levi overcome his inability to get enough nourishment from his food to help him grow.

The protocol was quite complex and took a lot of maintenance. It called for a diet of high calories and a supplement of four cans of Pedia-Sure in addition to his regular meals.

Then, besides a more nourishing diet, we looked at

various occupational and physical therapies. I tried the mouth stimulation techniques that I had tried with the older FAS-affected kids. I used my finger to stimulate his palate and tongue, and gently rubbed the outside of his throat to induce a swallowing reflex.

Our greatest concern, however, was to watch out so that Levi wouldn't choke while eating. We had to feed him carefully because he had no sense of what he could safely put into his mouth, chew, and swallow.

I didn't dare give him a whole bowl of cereal. He would have tried to eat it all at once. Instead, I fed him, one Rice Krispie at a time.

For many months I also carried Levi in the same tummy sack next to my stomach. Both Harold and I held him for hours on end when he cried or suffered severe tremors. We took turns staying up all night with him during those early months of attachment and growth.

We tried to find the therapies that worked and help Levi with them. The major rehabilitation called for Sensory Integration, a set of therapies that tried to integrate the five senses.

The work with the sense of taste was interesting and helpful in dealing with the problems of his not being able to thrive from eating. The therapy called for introducing the toddler to sour, sweet, and spicy food tastes. It worked. A sour pickle was a way to wake up his senses.

Levi continues with speech therapy that helps him

learn how to speak but also deals with his tongue thrusting and other mouth problems.

His charts said that Levi has good gross motor skills but is lacking with his fine motor skills. (Gross motor skills are the basic ones—walking, running, jumping, maintaining balance, and holding on to something big like a basketball. Fine motor skills are for things like holding a pencil, drinking from a cup, picking up food with a spoon, and coloring with crayons.)

Levi also suffers from a lack of coordination between his brain and his body and sometimes gets confused and doesn't quite know how to respond. He learned by accident that he could refocus his brain by stopping and putting his thumb in his mouth. After watching that activity I found myself using it to help him focus when he was acting erratic or losing control— I just tell him, "Thumb it, Levi. Use your thumb." He immediately gets the idea and puts the thumb in his mouth—and that somehow subdues the unfocused energy or controls the emotion that was getting out of hand. It was an interesting and amazing little discovery.

In the year that he has been with us we have seen remarkable progress. I'm glad that we didn't go ahead with the permanent feeding tube. The therapies are working, and he is able to eat more normally now and although he is still very tiny compared to other children his age, Levi is steadily improving.

I often look back to that day when the policeman found Levi in the trash and I am overwhelmed by God's grace. It was a real miracle that Levi survived. It was an "impossible" situation. Yet I believe that God saved Levi for a purpose and one day we will get to see that purpose fulfilled.

CHAPTER TWELVE

Zachary Ngozi-Bandele

I shared some of the story of our most recent adoption in the first few pages of chapter one of this book. It was the coming of Zachary into our lives. By way of review, I'm going to repeat some of the story in order to bring our story up-to-date and finish it.

Zachary's story began for us in October 1998 when I got a phone call from an adoption organization that I help. I thought I'd misunderstood the voice on the other end of the telephone. "What did you say?" I asked.

"It's true! The hospital nurse overheard them talking. She heard the father say that he was actually planning to *kill their newborn baby!*"

The hair on the back of my neck stood up as my mind tried to grasp the horror of such an act of violence.

The telephone call was from my friend, Margaret

Fleming. Margaret is the director of Adopt Link, an adoption agency in Chicago that specializes in adoptions of African-American and biracial babies and children.

"Oh, Patty," Margaret continued, "this is a travesty!" Then as she explained I began to understand the story more clearly. A baby boy was born without lower arms and legs. The baby had a few other medical concerns as well, but otherwise appeared to be a strong and healthy little guy.

The baby's parents were Nigerian and had won the Nigerian national lottery so that's why they were in the United States. While in America the mother learned that she was pregnant and so the baby was born in a Chicago hospital.

However, after the baby was born and the parents learned about his severe limb impairments, they became overwhelmed with grief. They knew that they would be expected to follow their cultural practices and if they did, it would require a most difficult decision on their part.

That's when the nurse overheard the father order his wife to get dressed so that they could leave the hospital.

"But she can't leave now," the nurse explained. "Your wife has had a very difficult breech birth—she must stay until we make sure that her bleeding has stopped, at least overnight."

"No," the man said bluntly, "we must leave at once.

It is the custom."

"Custom?" the nurse asked.

"When a baby is born like this, with deformities, it is an evil omen. The child must not be allowed to live."

"Uh—what exactly do you mean?" the nurse asked him. Astonished, she could hardly believe such a thing could happen in this day in America. "When you say that your baby must not be allowed to live, do you mean you are going to *kill him?*"

"Yes, it is a part of our culture," the man replied in a matter-of-fact way.

"But you can't do that in our country! That's murder! It's against the laws of our land," the nurse told him excitedly.

The couple seemed confused by that information, but the husband was quite firm in the decision to take his wife and the baby and leave the hospital. The baby's father left the room and left the ordeal of decision up to the mother (whose Nigerian name I later learned was Iyapo[1]). Iyapo was crying, almost as if it was clear that she did not want to be a part of the cultural decision to end the baby's life, but must have felt that she had no choice.

When the nurse told her supervisor, a quick call was made to the Social Service Agency and they quickly intervened. A welfare worker met with the Nigerian

---

[1]The name means "many trials, many difficult situations."

couple and explained U.S. laws and told the parents that they could not harm the baby in any way. After some dialogue, a compromise was worked out—the couple could leave, but *without* the baby. They surrendered the child to the adoption agency and gave up all their parental rights to their newborn son.

Those were the bizarre events that had preceded my urgent telephone call from Margaret. As she was telling me the story, my thoughts flashed back many years to my own time in Africa. I had gone as a girl with my parents who were medical missionaries to the Republic of Congo. I knew it was the custom of many African tribes to sacrifice a baby born with severe birth defects. It is considered an evil omen—and it's always said to be the fault of the mother. Sometimes it is even thought that an evil spirit impregnated the mother in the first place. In any event, the baby is killed and the mother mutilates herself as part of the grieving process. It seemed strange to hear of such a thing happening in a modern city like Chicago, though.

"Patty, do you have any families on your list that might be willing to consider adopting this special-needs baby?" Margaret was asking as my mind came back from its mental detour to Africa.

I was surprised at the first words out of my mouth. "Margaret," I said, "of course I know of someone who will take this baby. You're talking about *my* son! *We'll* take him."

My husband Harold walked into the room just then and I put my hand over the phone and said to him, "Honey, our baby boy has just been born in Chicago."

Harold looked at me with a slightly odd expression, then smiled. "Really?" he said with a bemused expression that seemed to say, "Here we go again!"

I got more information from Margaret concerning the baby. "The couple has been in the United States for most of the mother's pregnancy. She got good prenatal care and even had three ultrasound exams. But all three ultrasounds were read incorrectly to indicate that a normal baby boy was going to be born. None of the doctors saw that the baby was missing its arms and legs," Margaret explained.

I shuddered. Had they seen the birth defects there is no doubt that the baby would have been aborted.

"Wow, Margaret," I said, "God saved this baby's life not once but three times."

I wrote down the other information and made hurried plans to drive to Chicago (an eight-hour trip each way) to meet with the mother and pick up the baby.

I called Dr. Heitsch to set up an appointment for a checkup when we returned from Chicago. Dr. Heitsch seemed excited for me after I explained what was happening. "We'll need to send over a lactation specialist before you leave," she told me.

"A what?" I asked.

"A lactation specialist," she repeated. "You are going to breast-feed the baby, aren't you?"

"At my age? You're not serious," I replied. I could tell from the silence on the other end of the phone that she was serious. "Really?" I asked. "Is such a thing possible?"

"Yes, it is possible."

"But, Grace, I always thought that nursing was a by-product of pregnancy—that a mother's milk came in after childbirth," I said.

"That's not quite the way it works," the pediatrician said. "I'm going to fit you with a device that will get the baby to suck. The device is like a necklace with really tiny tubes that are taped to your nipple. When the baby sucks, milk will come out of the tube that goes into the corner of his mouth when he sucks at your nipple. After a week or two, your body's hormones will have been tricked into creating milk of its own."

"How does that work?" I asked.

"Well," she answered, "it isn't the pregnancy, or sucking, or any of those things by themselves. It's a matter of psychological energy and bonding with that helpless infant that causes the right hormones to be manufactured and produce the milk."

"That's remarkable," I told her.

"There's a great side effect of nursing your baby, too," Dr. Heitsch added. "In addition to breast milk being better nutrition and helping the infant build his immune system, nursing creates special hormones that actually alleviate stress. You'll appreciate that aspect."

I met with the lactation specialist that night before I was to leave for Chicago and she taught me how to use the breast-feeding device.

"It might take a while," she explained, "but your milk will come in eventually. So don't be concerned and worry about it. It'll happen."

I left the next morning for Chicago. The autumn foliage was in its peak as I traveled the interstate toward Illinois. The fall colors were evident on oaks, maples, birch, and sumac. It was like a visual symphony and the trip was almost a relaxing diversion instead of an urgent assignment.

When I got to Chicago I was thankful for the opportunity to talk with the biological mother.

I introduced myself and asked if there was anything I could do for her. "Would you like me to keep your names and address so that when he is older your baby can contact you if he wants to?" I asked.

"No," Iyapo said quickly. "I do not want him to ever know me. I have brought shame upon him and to my family," she added. It was obvious that in addition to suffering the grief and loss of having to give up her baby she was also tortured by guilt and shame.

"That isn't so," I reassured her. "It isn't your fault that he was born that way." *If anything,* I thought to myself, *it's the father's genes that carry this birth defect trait.* But I didn't say it. I only repeated that it wasn't her fault.

"You know," I continued, "maybe God allowed him to be born this way to touch the lives of many, many people. I believe that God has a genuine purpose for this baby and that's why He has protected him."

I asked Iyapo if I could have her picture and show the baby when he grows up. She responded firmly. "No! He cannot know anything about me."

In her sad voice I could hear the silent cries of a mother who cared deeply but because of her culture could not keep the baby that she had lovingly carried for nine months.

She hesitated "I know the same God as you," Iyapo explained in a quiet voice, "but my husband and my family must not know." Then she took a small orange book out of her purse. "I will leave one gift for him," she said, sadly knowing that it would be the only connection the child would ever have with his biological mother. The precious little gift was a Gideon New Testament that she had been given.

The mother and I seemed to have an immediate affinity for each other, so I took a chance that my words would not offend her. "Would you mind if I prayed for you?" I asked her.

She whispered, "Please do." I prayed that God would honor the choice that had been made for them to save the life of their son. I prayed for God to continue to watch over the baby as well as his parents, and look after this dear woman and protect her from any cultural animosity or trouble. As I prayed I could sense the warmth of her spirit. When I finished my prayer, there was an affection and gratitude and an instant bonding between us. I will forever hold that moment in my heart.

Since the couple had not named the baby I asked if it was all right with them if I chose a name. "I have three names in addition to our surname," I explained. "I'd like to give him the biblical name of Zachary which means 'God hath remembered.' I think that name is significant because God did remember him and kept him from harm. The second name is African—Ngozi, which means 'a blessing.' The third name, Bandele, is also African and means 'born away from home.' What do you think?"

Iyapo wept with joy as she approved the name, thanking me for keeping part of Zachary's heritage alive by giving him an African name.

It took almost a month to care for the paperwork and

work out the details between the states of Illinois and Wisconsin that would permit me to take Zachary home with me. I stayed with my daughter Jennifer and her husband in Chicago while we waited. I'm sure it was odd for her to have a newborn living with them for those weeks.

Zachary took to breast-feeding right away and usually woke up at two A.M. for a feeding. I was grateful for the suggestion of Dr. Heitsch to breast-feed as it helped me to bond more quickly with Zachary.

Everywhere we went people adored him. A baby who had no limbs initially intrigued other people, but the impairment never made him inferior. In almost every other respect he is a relatively healthy baby boy. He has a gentle and happy disposition and loves the attention he gets from other moms and grandmothers.

When we got back to Wisconsin, Zachary was loved immediately by everyone in the family. The older girls wanted to hold him and sing to him. Ari, unable to move, asked me to put his infant carrier on the table in front of her wheelchair so that she could watch him.

Zachary must have reminded Ari of her former crib-mate Sameer who was also limb deficient. "When you get big, Zachary," Ari cooed, "I'll tell you how to get around. My friend Sameer could crawl even without legs, so we'll help you learn how to get around, too."

In one of her other "conversations" with Zachary I heard Ari say to him, "You know, Zachary, you'll just have to learn how to do things differently. I had to do that because I can't move my arms and legs yet. When I came from India I had to learn new ways of doing things, too. They call that 'physical therapy' and at first I thought Mom was mean because it was so hard to do. But I learned that it helped me, so if it seems like Mom and Dad are mean when they make you do those exercises, they really aren't."

I had to bite my lip as my eyes filled at hearing her pep talk for Zachary.

In April of this year I took Zachary to St. Joseph's Hospital for a series of tests. Ari came with us for more tests for her surgery planned for August. We stayed in a Ronald McDonald House across from the hospital.

One of the instructions given by the hospital was that Zachary was not to have any food or water after ten P.M. until the next morning at ten A.M. because it would interfere with the accuracy of the tests. I knew that was going to be a problem because Zachary was only six months old and we couldn't explain why he couldn't be nursed when he awakened as usual at two A.M. Not wanting to waken the rest of those staying at the Ronald McDonald House with his crying, I took Zachary for a walk. Nearby was a cemetery so we walked through the cemetery for three hours as I sang softly to him, trying to soothe him.

A police car came by during this time and shined a spotlight on us. The officer got out and called, "Are you all right, ma'am?" I assured him that I was and explained our dilemma. He smiled and told me to be careful and drove off.

At eight o'clock in the morning I took Zachary for the tests. He was still crying with hunger and lack of sleep, but the tests were done and I immediately nursed him.

Later that afternoon I took him to a specialist to examine him for future prostheses. The doctor ordered X-rays of his remnant limbs to determine the amount of bone structure.

One of the consulting surgeons told us that he recommended amputation of the limbs to remove the little buds that should have developed into hands and feet, with fingers and toes. The idea behind this was to make wearing of artificial arms and legs more comfortable.

But amputation sounded so final so I asked them to wait. Later, while we were waiting in the office of Dr. Jacobson for Ari to be examined, a friend who was with me mentioned a plastic surgeon in Illinois who had performed a remarkable reattachment of a hand on a little boy. "You know, if that kind of surgery can be done, why wouldn't it be possible for them to transplant the foot buds with those little toes to the arms so Zachary can use them as fingers?"

We told Dr. Jacobson about the idea. "Interesting concept," he said as he came over to look at Zachary. Then he said, "Just a minute. I'm going to call in a colleague who's an expert in plastic and microsurgery. Let's see what he says."

A few minutes later the other surgeon came in and examined Zachary. "There are nerves and tendons present in both sets of limbs," he observed. "The left side is better on both the arm and leg, and the right side is also consistent. I think it might work."

The doctors suggested that we wait until Zachary was about two years old to do the operation, and meanwhile, they would fit him with artificial arms and legs.

Zachary continues to amaze us with what he can do with just portions of limbs. He has learned to hold a bottle and how to move around on the floor. He has incredible strength in his back and trunk to compensate for his limb deficiencies.

He also continues to charm people wherever he goes. One day when I stopped at a garage sale I noticed a little boy staring at Zachary. Since small children are intrigued because Zachary has no arms or legs, I bent down with Zachary in my arms and asked the little boy, "Would you like to see the baby?"

The boy looked at Zachary then gazed up at me.

"Your baby is different," he said simply.

I nodded and went into a long narrative about how sometimes babies are born different and waited for his follow-up questions.

The boy kept looking at Zachary and repeated, "He's different."

"Yes," I said smiling. "You are a very bright little boy. I'm glad that you can see that God makes everybody different."

The little three-year-old nodded. "Yeah, him different 'cause he got curly hair."

Both his mom and I laughed. We both had guessed that the boy was talking about Zachary's limb deficiency or perhaps his dark skin color. But the boy saw only that the baby had curly hair as contrasted with his blond straight hair.

Recently I read the journal entry that I had written on the day I picked up Zachary:

October 19, 1998
My beautiful baby Zachary,
    My world stood still the moment I held you . . .it was as if our souls had always been connected even though I did not give birth to you.
    I must be the luckiest mom in the world to

*have been given such a wonderful gift! I will
be forever grateful to your birth mother who
carried you for nine months, then grieved for
you and her loss. Somehow our spirits touched
and one day I will tell you of her. You are a
special boy and I love you so.*

*Daddy and I chose to give you an African
name, which pleased your birth mom. We
wanted you to keep a part of Africa with you.
Maybe one day I will take you to the Africa
that I love and show you the land that had
such a significant impact in my life. Until
then, little one, I shall tell you all the stories
that I know about your heritage. Daddy and I
will celebrate who you are as we do with each
child in our family.*

*God has a very special plan for you, little
one. He sent His guardian angels to protect
you. Daddy and I are honored to have been
selected to love and raise you. Our journey
together has just begun! Rest peacefully,
my son. Mommy and Daddy are right by
your side.*

As Zachary moves closer to his first birthday, we are all
grateful to God—more than ever—for this wonderful

baby and the great blessing that he has brought to our family.

Zachary is always cheerful and spreads that happiness to the rest of the family. If one of the children is having a difficult time with therapy or suffers from seizures or mood swings, Zachary can invariably cheer him up.

He does have special needs—some hearing loss, mild kidney problems, and asthma—but to us he is perfect in every way! He has a quick mind and I truly expect that God has an unusually wonderful plan for Zachary when he grows up. It's exciting to even think about it now.

Chapter Thirteen

Butting Heads with Bureaucrats

The social services caseworker had gotten the birth mother of Zachary to sign the documents surrendering her child to the state so that adoption proceedings could follow quickly.

This was when things began to get complicated. I was told that because the baby was born in Illinois but we lived in Wisconsin, it fell to the Interstate Compact to approve the placement and supervise the adoption. It was formed to keep matters like ours from "falling between the cracks" when a child goes from one state to another. The Interstate Compact is the agency that also commissions and reviews home studies of the adoptive couple. In addition, it deals with the legal aspects of the adoption and coordinates the two sets of state policies and procedures.

One matter that wasn't resolved was: How were Zachary's medical bills going to be met? The State of Wisconsin, where we lived, no doubt would have preferred that Illinois care for these expenses, since that is where the baby was born. Wisconsin no doubt saw Zachary as a taxpayer's nightmare. As a special-needs baby, the medical costs were likely to be great.

We were unaware of another wrinkle. It had to do with the fact that Zachary's parents voluntarily surrendered their baby to the state instead of going through a lengthy process and a hearing to determine the termination of parental rights. The practical difference was a serious consideration for us. When children are taken and put into the foster-care system and parental rights are terminated, the children are eligible for an adoption subsidy to help with the unusual medical expenses. However, because Zachary was *surrendered voluntarily* by his parents, he did not qualify for the medical subsidy, according to the State of Illinois. That's why the State of Wisconsin was concerned about the potential cost to taxpayers if something were to happen to Harold and me.

I was told that one way to qualify Zachary for the subsidy was to institutionalize him for four to six months. But I wasn't willing to do that—after all, those are the most critical months in a child's life for attachment and bonding. Babies have a window of about nine months to attach or bond with their first caregiver. If they are institutionalized they never learn how to be socially interactive. If no one comes to care for the baby when it needs to be fed or changed, the baby will eventually stop crying when no one comes to check on it.

They never learn to smile because there is no one to smile at them.

By the time they are old enough for school, these children with attachment disorder have never been taught the benefits of doing what other people want. As a result the child doesn't follow the "rules of society" and obey. Eventually that child becomes sociopathic and confused. The worst of these kids end up in jail by age thirteen. They have never been taught that you have to behave in order to be cared for in society. That, as I see it, is the kind of problem created when policy is more important than the child.

I wasn't going to sacrifice Zachary's well-being just to meet some policy. Besides, I was also breast-feeding him, which I felt was another important consideration, so these reasons made the idea of institutionalizing him unacceptable.

Zachary and I had to stay in Chicago for three weeks while the Interstate Compact tried to work things out between Illinois and Wisconsin. Until they were able to iron out these differences, I was not allowed to return to

Wisconsin with the baby.

I had to hire a private attorney to argue that Zachary should qualify for the medical assistance. It seemed so foolish to me. I'd think that states would want to *encourage* special-needs adoptions by helping with the medical expenses. One child adopted means the state is relieved of $25,000 to $90,000—*every year!*—money that the state will have to pay for that child's support (if it is not adopted).

Looking at it another way, statistics tell us that special-needs children who are institutionalized and not adopted are many times more likely to end up in prison as adults. The cost for housing a typical prison inmate is $75,000 a year or more.

Yet, we still had to argue with them for medical assistance. It was to no avail; we were turned down. We took our case all the way to Washington where Donna Shalala's office (the U.S. Department of Health and Human Services) was sympathetic but could not do anything because of states' rights. My only consolation was that I was able to bring these issues to the attention of more pragmatic policymakers.

In the end I had to sign an agreement acknowledging the baby's high risk and agreeing to obtain our own medical insurance for him. We're still hoping that the State of Illinois, where Zachary was born, will acknowledge its obligation and provide us that adoption subsidy for medical help.

Our experience with Interstate Compact was not an isolated case, however. Here are some excerpts from a letter written to me from Debbie and Tom Schmitz, another Wisconsin couple. They detail their own private nightmare:

> *Our other three adoptions were within the State of Wisconsin so we knew nothing of how complicated things can be when two states are incompatible. Our baby was born in North Carolina and didn't have some of the same rules of terminating rights of the biological parents. The birth parents were a married couple who surrendered their rights. Little did we know that this would be our nightmare.*
>
> *Wisconsin would not recognize the voluntary surrender. . .so the parents would need to terminate in Wisconsin's court system. The (North Carolina) agency felt this was asking too much of the parents as they were still grieving the adoption of their baby.*
>
> *Daily the decisions changed! Then they said we couldn't have the baby! I was hysterical. I called Patty, sobbing.*

> *Patty reassured me and gave me the num-*
> *bers to contact. We started with congressmen*
> *and ended with a lawyer.*

Debbie and Tom encountered other "glitches" in the process of trying to work with two different states in completing that adoption. Fortunately the telephone calls were effective. The Wisconsin agency took a commonsense approach to the problem instead of simply quoting policy. And there was a happy ending—Debbie and Tom had the joy of holding their new daughter in their arms and seeing the adoption completed.

How I wish more adoptions could be done.

Because of policies like these, I began to be an advocate for special-needs children shortly after we adopted Ari. I have been traveling, speaking, and telephoning all over the country to communicate for those who otherwise aren't being heard.

I believe that my advocacy has stepped up several notches since Zachary was born. Butting heads with bureaucracies and their outdated policies has helped to open doors for better consideration of special-needs babies. I have been invited to speak on that issue before Congress, and this year I will be attending a conference of all Interstate Compacts. That conference will address ways to understand how the processes of state governments affect those of other states, especially in those areas where I have tried to raise national consciousness, such as providing medical subsidies for special-needs kids, or improving Medicaid coverage.

I have also found myself advocating for special-needs youngsters in other ways. For example, one state recently passed a law to limit family size of foster-care and adoptive families. It used to be agency policy that families with eight or more in them could not do foster care or adopt. That policy has now become law in that state and has arbitrarily reduced the size of the family that can do foster care or adopt children to six people in a family—and only three of these can be special-needs children.

Bureaucracy says that if you have more than six children you can't be a good and effective parent. Bureaucracy says that the most important thing is the number of bathrooms you have in your house—the number of board feet, number of windows, and the number of bedrooms that qualify you to be a good parent.

My "crusade" is for common sense to dictate policy, using a single guideline: *What is in the best interest of the children?*

I agree that eight might be too many for some families. But the consideration should be made on a case-by-case basis. There should be only one criterion: *Are the kids thriving in this home?* If so, then the social workers should use common sense in deciding on whether another child can be placed in a large family.

Those of us that have large families with special-needs children have learned a great deal about helping these youngsters. This experience is valuable and it's valid regardless of family size. It's true that some families of more than eight people might be stretched. But for the most part, the large family is what helps make the program work.

Dr. Grace Heitsch mentioned something that I've never forgotten. She has observed our (large) family in many different situations. Grace told me that it was amazing to her to see how our older kids take responsibility and help the younger ones. Helping Mom or Dad makes them feel good about themselves—they feel needed. When any child (whether special needs or normal) *feels needed,* their self-image improves significantly. Not only that, kids who feel needed have a sense of belonging and attachment.

To have the state come in and regulate the size of the foster-care or adoptive family seems rather draconian to me. I have never heard of any such laws to regulate the size of families for drug addicts or alcoholics who produce babies—most of them born addicts—almost on a yearly basis (such as Levi's birth mother who gave birth to *seven* special-needs babies). Laws regulating family size remind me of the totalitarian limits on family size imposed on couples in China.

It wasn't the choice of the foster parent that the mother of the child was an addict and the baby was born addicted to crack cocaine and alcohol. These children are problems of society. As society *we all need to take care of them.* We need to provide enough money for professional, qualified, and accountable foster parents.

The overwhelming majority of foster parents are not in it for the money. Most could do better financially at other jobs—even flipping hamburgers at the local fast-food chain at minimum wage. I could go back to work for a hospital or dental office (as I did before we began doing foster care) and make a great deal more money than the stipend that state agencies pay foster parents to care for children.

Just compare the salary of a hospital professional in a supervisory role with the eleven dollars a day that agencies pay foster-care parents to take full-time care of a child. That works out to *forty-five cents an hour!* From this amount they are also expected to buy food and clothing for the child. It costs more than eleven dollars to hire a teenage baby-sitter to watch a "normal" child while the husband and wife go out for dinner *for just three hours.*

Despite the extremely low pay, we expect foster parents to be qualified, thoroughly trained, and experts on all issues regarding normal and special-needs children. It doesn't make sense.

Though a small minority, too many are uneducated and too poor to do anything else for a living. If they are working for the subsidy that only having a large number of kids makes cost-effective, they are not working for the benefit of the children. I suspect that it is this kind of abuse of the system that created the policy against large families, but it is one that can be easily solved by dealing with it on a case-by-case basis rather than legislating arbitrarily against large families.

Nonetheless, it seems crazy to me that any state would want to penalize the one segment of society that can help. I shudder to think of what's going to happen to special-needs kids in the future. It is already very difficult to find foster-care or adoptive parents for special-needs children.

Another policy that I have taken to task with several agencies is their bias against older adoptive parents. I remember when I was interviewed by the agency for our overseas adoption of Ari how this bias came through in the questions.

"Okay," the interviewer said to me then, "I have just a few questions to fill out on my form. Could I have your age, please?"

"I'm in my forties," I generalized.

"Uh, well, that's a little old—but I think we can still work with that," she said. "And your husband's age?"

"Well, let's see," I answered, "he was fifty-(mumble) on his last birthday so that means he'll be (mumble) next month."

"What is his date of birth, Mrs. Anglin?" Reluctantly, because I already knew what her response would be, I told her.

"But he'll be *sixty* next month!" the woman said with the same level of incredulity as if I'd said I was married to Methuselah.

"I'm sorry," she continued, "your husband is way too old."

"But you *have* to work with us," I told her.

"Sorry; it's our policy."

"Wait a minute. Do you do single-parent adoptions?" I asked her.

"Yes, we do, but—"

"Well, if you do single-parent adoptions, then just consider my husband dead," I suggested.

"We can't do that," she argued.

"But you've already written him off anyway," I reminded her. "What is your reasoning behind your bias against age?"

She replied, "We don't want to have the children face the loss of a parent down the road."

"And you don't think that *not being adopted* won't give them a sense of loss?" I responded.

I am glad to say that the agency did make an exception to their policy about age and took the matter to their board for consideration (a perfect example of what I mean by commonsense reasoning instead of arbitrary rules). We got them to change their minds and we adopted Ari. Since then, we have adopted four more children in spite of our "ancient" ages.

Unfortunately, many agencies make no exceptions to their policies and countless children are deprived of the benefit of a valuable, untapped resource. People whose children are grown now have more time, money, and attention to give to the rearing of children.

Older or retired couples make great parents. They often have experience of having raised children already and are less likely to make the mistakes they made as younger parents. They usually have more wisdom, insight, and maturity as well. Interestingly, Eastern cultures recognize and respect age as a virtue. I wish that our culture were as open.

In our situation, Harold—because he is retired— has more time for the children. He is a full-time parent and can even "out-mom" me if he wants to. He cooks, changes diapers, serves meals, disciplines, teaches in our homeschool, and provides one-to-one attention to any of the children who need it. If Harold still had a nine-to-five job, he'd be gone during most of the kids' critical waking hours.

I have worked long and hard to try to change those policies about older foster parents and adoptive couples and I hope that we are making some headway.

Most of the problems that we run into are caused by policymakers and not by the "hands-on" social workers in the trenches. The caseworkers usually have common sense born of their experience, but they are forced to "go by the book" with an outdated or impractical policy rather than finding creative ways to work things out. Blanket policies can never effectively be used to evaluate and improve the lives of other human beings.

I am a strong believer in judging each child and every family on a case-by-case basis. The "one size fits all" style of social welfare does not work in our day.

I also believe that judges, attorneys, and social workers should be qualified. It is one thing to have the requisite number of credit hours of schooling but quite another to have practical experience in decisions that affect a child.

Before a person can be a teacher he or she must practice (intern) teaching. We also have internships for doctors. Why do we not expect it of someone who has the power to permanently decide the outcome of someone's *lifetime?* Those dealing with the fates of children are not even required to have a minimum number of credit hours in child psychology.

In my opinion judges, attorneys, and social workers should have a requirement which says that before they can make any decisions affecting a child's life they must have at least one year as a foster parent. That "internship" will give them practical experience and help them understand the impact that their decisions can have.

Most of those in positions of power and making decisions have never done foster care. In fact, many of them have said to me, "I don't know how you do it. I could never do that." Yet they so quickly and easily assume that a thirteen- or fifteen-year-old child/mom can do a good job!

I find that most social-welfare and child-agency workers like what I am doing and often go out of their way to encourage or thank me. For the most part they have my respect and admiration. We are more likely to see eye-to-eye on matters.

It's the policymakers of these agencies that are not as kindly toward me. I suppose it's because I often challenge the status quo and question their blanket policies. I truly don't do it to be a troublemaker. It's just that I have taken on the responsibility to act for the ultimate good of the children.

In my advocacy for the children I often feel like I'm walking a tightrope. There are so many things to say and do to help special-needs children, but many of these things call for pointing out weaknesses and bad policies in the various governmental bodies. Sometimes I feel like all I'm doing is butting heads with bureaucracy. Yet, other times I think I see some progress.

I always want to be careful in dealing with people in authority who have the power to do things that might jeopardize the children's welfare. It is never wise to stir things up and cause more problems than solutions.

My work with special-needs children has also opened doors of opportunity to bring these problems before powerful people in authority. I am the chairman of Children's Health Alliance of Wisconsin and work with families and agencies across the state to solve child health issues and lobby for better state involvement in providing health and dental care for children.

In my role as regional coordinator for Adopt America Network I have helped hundreds of families to connect with babies or children like ours to adopt.

Adopt America was formed in 1983 and every year matches hundreds of special-needs babies and children to the adoptive parents who will care for them. Interested families find out about the program and call or write me and I put them in touch with Adopt America that has photos and résumés for prospective adoptive parents to review.

I just received a letter from a couple that I had helped that shows something of the process and the joy that results when a child and a family are brought together. The family has given me their permission to share excerpts of their letter:

Dear Patty,

In 1997 Tom and I started our long, frustrating adoption process. We knew that God wanted us to adopt a child with Down's syndrome. . .but we felt we needed to wait until our birth children were older. Jon had turned twelve and Erika was almost ten and we felt it was the perfect time to introduce another child into our family.

In February 1999 we met you, Patty, and we knew that you were sent to us from God to help us. You called our social worker and advocated on our behalf and she agreed to finish up the home study as soon as possible. We faxed it to you from the office. Much to our wonder you then faxed it to the agency that was handling the baby and they were able to present us to the parents (of a Down's syndrome baby girl). We later learned that we were one of eight couples applying. By the time we got home that evening you had called and told us that we were the family that the birth parents had chosen and that they had known without a doubt we were the couple that God wanted to raise their child! Isn't God good?

We met Maarja on April 20, 1999, the day after her birth and we were able to take her home the following day right from the hospital. We all instantly fell in love with her; the name Maarja means "desired child" in Swedish. We know that God is going to use her life to touch a lot of people.

We know the sacrifices that you and your family have made for us both in time and money and we are truly grateful. Thank you so much for listening to God's voice and being willing to be used of Him. We are also so glad that we have been able to get to know you and Harold and your family. We know you will be lifetime friends.

> *Forever grateful,*
> *Tom, Kirsten, Jon, Erika, & Maarja*

It usually takes six months to a year to complete the

process of adopting a special-needs baby or child, but Tom and Kirsten and their family know that it is truly a worthwhile experience.

In addition to working for these two fine organizations I also get opportunities to address my concern for adopting special-needs kids when I speak in churches. I'm sometimes asked to appear at churches to talk about the problems, but I also make it a point to speak to those sincere advocates who are out on the picket lines promoting the Right to Life cause. I remind them that I approve of their noble efforts to save the lives of the unborn, but I also ask those who oppose abortion—*What are you doing to help with the problem of the unwanted children who ARE born?* The problem of these special-needs children are just as vital to God and, like abortion, has become a huge political question.

Churches can be a tremendous part of the solution to these unwanted children. Jesus told us to look after the children, widows, and orphans. We *all* need to take responsibility for the problem and be part of its solution.

Not everyone will be called to adopt eight special-needs children as we have done. But maybe God would have you consider adopting *one such child*. Or, if even that commitment intimidates you, why not become foster parents for a year or so? You'll recall that is how we became interested in the first place. By being foster parents you can do some good while you "try out" the idea of being parents to a special boy or girl.

Harold and I feel that God has given us a tremendous calling and He has equipped us for it. It hasn't always been easy but it certainly has been rewarding. Our experiences have given us opportunities to be on the cutting edge of what I feel is an exciting new ministry.

I invite you to reach out in love to a needy child and give that little boy or girl something valuable—*love* and *hope*.

My Dream for Acres of Hope

People often wonder how a large family like ours functions and ask how I am able to get so much done. Recently someone wrote that she could not imagine how I can take care of *eight* special-needs children, let alone handle all my other activities. I guess that these "other activities" do sound rather imposing—working with two agencies, spending time on the phone, counseling, speaking in churches, and traveling.

My advocacy involvements could easily be full-time work if I let it. But I have learned that I have to carefully manage my time.

My greatest secret is that I have a wonderful partner and so many "assistants" to help me be efficient. Harold, as I have said repeatedly, is a terrific dad to our children, but he is also a great "mom" as well. When I am busy on the telephone, taking the children to their medical appointments, or counseling prospective adoptive parents, he always jumps in and takes over the household duties.

I prove this again even as I write this. I am sitting in the parents' waiting room at St. Joseph's Hospital in Marshfield, Wisconsin. Harold has taken over the household duties while I am here with Ari, who is undergoing surgery again. She has just come through a ten-hour operation and I will likely be here for almost a week. But I know that Harold is capably handling everything at home.

Our children also pitch in. Each of them is taught from early childhood to assume responsibilities and chores. Often this involves helping to care for a younger sibling. It is through this process, as I have said, that they also strengthen their self-esteem. When I am gone they miss me, but it is not as much of an issue when Harold is there to reassure them.

Not only that, I always make it a point to take some of the children with me on my trips to board meetings, speaking engagements, and medical interventions. This time I have Zachary and T. J. with me. The last time Brian was the older child who came with me to help. Each of the boys is old enough to help me with the younger child or children that I bring with me, but it also gives us a chance for some real one-on-one quality time together.

During a previous three-hour drive to the hospital Brian and I had some wonderful conversations—the kind of talks mothers long for with their children—and I'm not sure that we'd have discussed those serious things at home.

Harold also takes one or more of the children along when he has to be away. The last time he took a trip Serina accompanied him.

I also take care not to be gone too long, either. And to provide balance, I make sure that when I am home that I am available to the children. Two weeks ago we had our annual "family camp" where we bring the whole family together for a week of fun—including the grown and married ones. This year we packed up everyone in our school bus, along with all their clothes for the week, and traveled to a rustic campground. It was a wonderful family reunion. Even though some of the children have grown and left home, every one of them will still offer to help if we need it. So I have over a dozen "assistants."

We also have a lot of friends and neighbors who volunteer to help. There are so many that I would need many pages just to thank them for their help.

I suppose I also have to credit my parents to a certain extent because I inherited their genes for good organizational skills.

As I sit here in the hospital waiting and praying for

Ari, I find myself thinking about the future. And there is one dream that keeps coming back into my thoughts. I alluded to it earlier but never fully explained it. My dream is for our farm to be a haven for children and used to help young mothers-to-be.

There are too many young girls who become pregnant and do not know how to take care of themselves or their unborn children. I keep thinking what might have happened if Iris's or Levi's biological mothers might have had someone to guide them, to look after them, give them a place to live during their pregnancy, steer them away from bad influences and habits, and help them learn how to be mothers.

There is a small building next to our house on the farm. It was previously used as a place to house cars and farm machinery. But I'd like to have it renovated into a two-bedroom cottage for a young mother-to-be. She could live there during her pregnancy and learn from us. There is a lot to learn from a large family like ours that works together. She can observe good role models and how to be a good mother. If she does not want to keep her baby, we can review applications and résumés of prospective adoptive parents together and make a decision regarding her baby without a lot of bureaucratic distractions.

The clean, country air and healthy food will be a

better preparation for the new baby's life than living in an unhealthy environment and being exposed to drugs and alcohol.

The farm will be far away from former friends and the negative peer pressures that make it so difficult for a troubled teen or young woman to overcome her addictions or associations.

I keep thinking about Iris who, as a thirteen-year-old girl, was much too young to be a mother. She was just a child herself and needed as much help as the babies that she gave up for adoption. She and I had a wonderful rapport. I believe that if she could have stayed with me at our Acres of Hope farm during her pregnancy, she might have learned some helpful principles and lessons that might have kept her from falling back into a terrible pattern of failure.

There are always other girls like Iris to be saved from making such awful choices and mistakes. My dream is to help them, one at a time, if that's all I can do. How I wish that Harold and I were able to somehow have the resources to build that cottage on our Acres of Hope and get started.

Maybe one day we will find a way.

Acres of Hope, Inc. is a 501(c) (3) non-profit charitable organization dedicated to providing educational information, emotional support, parent-to-parent support, advocacy services, financial assistance, and a loan program of items helpful to families dealing with children of physical and emotional challenges. In addition, our mission is to promote greater community understanding, acceptance, and support for families involved in adopting special-needs children cross-racially and cross-culturally.

For more information please contact:
Acres of Hope, Inc.
c/o Barbour Publishing, Inc.
PO Box 719
Uhrichsville, OH 44683

Visit our web site at www.acresofhope.com